How to Tip

Fodor'sfyi

Fodor's Travel Publications

New York • Toronto • London • Sydney • Auckland

www.fodors.com

How to Tip

Editors: Karen Cure, Melissa Klurman, Matthew Lombardi
Managing Editors: Robin Dellabough, Lisa DiMona, Karen Watts
Editorial Contributor: Rachel Hoyt
Production/manufacturing: Publications Development Company of Texas
Cover Design: Guido Caroti
Interior Design: Lisa Sloane

A Lark Production

ISBN: 1–4000–1158–2

Important Tip

Although all prices, opening times, and other details in this book are based on
information supplied to us at press time, changes occur all the time in the travel
world, and Fodor's cannot accept responsibility for facts that become outdated
or for inadvertent errors or omissions. So always confirm information when it
matters, especially if you're making a detour to visit a specific place.

Special Sales

Fodor's Travel Publications are available at special discounts for bulk purchases
for sales promotions or premiums. Special editions, including personalized
covers, excerpts of existing guides, and corporate imprints, can be created in
large quantities for special needs. For more information, contact your local
bookseller or write to Special Markets, Fodor's Travel Publications, 280 Park
Avenue, New York, NY 10017. Inquiries from Canada should be directed to
your local Canadian bookseller or sent to Random House of Canada, Ltd.,
Marketing Department, 2775 Matheson Boulevard East, Mississauga, Ontario
L4W 4P7. Inquiries from the United Kingdom should be sent to Fodor's Travel
Publications, 20 Vauxhall Bridge Road, London SW1V 2SA, England.

Printed in the United States of America

10 9 8 7 6 5 4 3 2 1

Contents

Tips on Tipping

MOST TIPPING IS, TECHNICALLY, OPTIONAL.
It's an act totally at your discretion—nothing's written in stone—you can do it or not do it. Yet there's no doubt that tipping greases the wheels of your travel and entertainment experience. Tipping can turn a rocky episode into a smooth one, or an average event into an extraordinary one. Why then do we struggle so much with the act of tipping?

Tipping anxiety is rooted in the fact that money matters make many people uncomfortable. Talking about money, bargaining, tipping—they're all in the same category of sticky subjects people would rather avoid. Tipping makes people uneasy precisely because there are no hard and fast rules—they don't know how much to tip or at what moment to tip, or even how to offer the tip in any given situation. Sure, figuring and filling in the tip amount on a restaurant credit card slip is easy enough, but what about the dozens of other tipping scenarios you encounter, especially when you travel? From bartenders to parking valets to maids to blackjack dealers—there are more people to tip than you can count on both hands, so where do you begin to get over the anxiety and get on with the tipping?

First, understand that tipping isn't charity; it's a business transaction. Many people employed in the service industry receive less than minimum wage and count on tipping to round out their wages so they can make a decent living. As the tipper, your role in the world-wide service economy is critical. Once you understand what's expected in tipping situations, the rest is simple math applied to the basic value of the services you have received. If you look at it in this practical way, it's easy to adjust the way you think about tipping.

So, plan to tip. People undertip or don't tip at all because they haven't planned in advance for the tipping opportunities they'll encounter when they travel. Plan for tipping as a portion of your travel expense, and plan to have ready cash to engage in tipping at all the appropriate moments. That doesn't mean micromanaging your travel experience, just having a good idea of how much to tip each party and enough small bills or change on hand to make it happen.

Understand that being a good tipper means being a smart tipper. You don't need to throw scads of greenbacks at people just because you feel you should tip something. If you learn how to tip appropriately, you won't be wasting your hard-earned money, and the people you are tipping will be properly compensated for services rendered.

Finally, recognize that tipping is your opportunity to express your pleasure or dissatisfaction with the service you receive. It is also an act of civility, an important gesture that shows your respect for the work of others. This book will show you how to make the most of every opportunity that arises in the business of tipping. The quality of your travel experience could depend on it.

The first three chapters of this book will introduce you to standard tipping practices that will come in handy throughout your travels in the United States; the fourth chapter will explain the rules for tipping at resorts, on cruises, and in casinos; and finally, the fifth chapter will detail the intricacies of tipping etiquette that you need to know before traveling to a foreign destination.

—The Editors

Tipping in Bars and Restaurants

FROM FANCY RESTAURANTS TO CORNER CAFÉS, from chic bars to hip dives, tipping the staff for good service is a customary part of dining and bar-going throughout the United States. As a rule, the more expensive the establishment, the more extensive the services—hence, the more people there are to tip. And, of course, the bigger the bill is, the bigger the tip will be. Although tipping amounts may vary from restaurant to restaurant and from bar to bar, it is a relief to know that tipping percentages and basic protocol are fairly standardized across the country. Keeping these standards in mind will help you plan your budget and avoid embarrassing tipping faux pas when you go out to eat or drink.

THE PRIMARY TIPS
Waiters and Waitresses

The most common occasion to tip in a restaurant is with the waitstaff. They're the people you'll encounter the most—and who should behave as your advocate—during your dining experience, so they'll get the lion's share of the tips. It's important to remember to tip the waitstaff based on the quality of the service, not the quality of the food. Bear in mind that although tipping waitstaff has virtually become a rule, not an option, the amount that you choose to tip can speak volumes about the service you've received.

What you tip your server is based on a percentage of your bill. A 15% tip has been the norm since the 1970s and is still considered acceptable today. In top-rate restaurants, however, a 20% tip is considered appropriate. The 20% tip is also a growing trend in larger cities such as New York and Los Angeles. If you're not sure what is customary, you can always ask when you're making a reservation.

SHARING THE WEALTH

Chances are the employee who did all the actual heavy lifting during your last restaurant outing wasn't the maître d' or the waiter—it was probably the busperson. The busperson keeps your water glass and the bread basket full, removes empty dishes, and refills your coffee cup, to name a few of the myriad tasks required during the course of a meal. The busperson is the waiter's right hand; when you tip the waiter at the end of the meal, you're also tipping the busperson, who usually ends up with 25% of the waiter's tip take.

You should expect any waiter or waitress to perform the following duties:

▶ Take your order at your seat when you're ready.

▶ Deliver your food and drink.

▶ Bring condiments and other extras—napkins, rolls—and refill drinks when needed. This shows she's been keeping her eye on your table.

▶ Check back to see if everything is all right or if you need anything else.

▶ Present the bill in a timely fashion at the end of the meal.

If these services are competently performed, a tip of at least 15% is warranted.

So, what are the circumstances for a reduced tip or no tip at all? These situations should be few and far between because bad staff won't last very long in the restaurant business. Once in a blue moon you'll come across truly bad service, but be realistic as to what defines "bad." If the waiter or waitress is belligerent and refuses to be of service to you, that's a no-tip situation. But, if the waiter accidentally spills tomato soup on you, immediately cleans it up, comps your lunch, and picks up the cleaning bill, do you skip the tip because he spilled the soup? Of course not.

Poor service, such as a server disappearing for a 15-minute break when you're looking for a drink refill, should be reflected in a reduced tip as opposed to no tip at all. After all, if you've gotten your meal, you've had *some* service, although perhaps not all you were expecting. Be sure to let either the server or the manager know why the tip was reduced so they can correct the situation and improve their service to customers. If you don't take the opportunity to express your dissatisfaction verbally, the message of your reduced tip may be lost. It's likely you'll just be thought of as a lousy tipper!

Always base your tip amount on the cost of the meal *before* taxes are added. You should be presented with an

O ne evening after particularly unsatisfying service at one of our area's nicer restaurants, I decided just leaving a 10% tip for the waiter instead of the customary 15% wasn't enough of a statement. How would our waiter know I undertipped him because he was forgetful and inattentive to our party if I

TRAVEL LOG didn't come right out and tell him? So I left a little note for him in the bill folder, telling him we enjoyed our meal but wished he had paid closer attention to our needs. I felt so much better expressing my complaint, and I like to think the waiter learned a little something, too.

—*Bill V., Phoenix, Arizona*

itemized bill so you can check it and figure the tip pretax. If your waitperson served you drinks from the bar or served your wine, include the costs of those items when figuring your tip. Use the tipping chart in the appendix of this book to help with your calculations.

Always tip the server at the end of the meal. When paying by credit card, fill in the tip amount on the credit slip. When paying by cash, give the tip to the server when you pay your bill or take the tip from your change and leave it on the table as you leave.

BEYOND THE CALL OF DUTY

Sometimes you'll encounter waitstaff who make your dining experience a delight. Here are some actions that you may want to tip extra for:

☐ Helping you off and on with your coat.

☐ Taking extra care or help with seating elderly or physically challenged diners in your group.

☐ Spending time explaining the menu and answering any questions.

☐ Communicating with the kitchen staff to make sure you get exactly what you want.

☐ Helping you choose the meal or wine that lets you get the most out of your dining experience.

Bartenders

An overly busy bar, or customer confusion when moving from the bar area to the dining area of a restaurant, can result in the barkeep getting the slip on the tip. Whether you're running a tab or paying per drink, be sure to take care of the bartender before moving on.

Calculate a bartender's tip either on a percentage of the final bill or on a per-drink basis. If you're tipping based on the total bill, figure on a 10% to 15% tip. Use the higher percentage if the bartender is being particularly attentive; 15% is appropriate when the bartender is running a tab for you, you're paying by credit card, or your tab is being transferred to the dining room.

When you're at a bar that is not part of a restaurant, you may want to up the percentage to 15% or 20%. Add an extra 5% to the tip if the bartender relays messages for you or gives you a phone to use.

If you're tipping by the drink, whether in a freestanding bar or in a bar that's part of a restaurant, leave at least $1 per drink. You can leave that after you get your change, or just round up the total by $1 and hand it to the bartender when you're paying. You can always leave more than $1 if you've been well taken care of.

Tip in cash when paying the total tab in cash or if you're leaving a tip after each drink. When paying by credit card, add the tip to the total bill.

If the bartender offers you a free drink, don't just say thanks and leave it at that. Always tip on a free drink. The usual tip would be about half of the cost of the drink, or more if you feel like it. You can always offer to buy the bartender a drink in return, but if she refuses, you should leave the tip anyway.

Cocktail Waiters and Waitresses

Like their colleagues in the dining room, cocktail waiters and waitresses should be tipped according to the service they provide. If they are only taking your order and bringing the drinks, a 10% tip is fine. If they bring you goodies like nuts, pretzels, or chips and salsa to nosh on, if they transfer your tab to the dining room, or if you're paying by credit card, 15% is sufficient. In establishments that have no restaurant area, a 15% tip is customary.

In restaurants, always leave the tip for the cocktail waiter or waitress before you leave or head off to your dining table.

OTHER POTENTIAL TIPS

As you move up the ladder to fine dining, there is a whole host of other tipping opportunities. You may not encounter all of these situations, but knowing how to handle them can help make for a better dining experience.

Maître d'

A restaurant maître d' is often a salaried management position and therefore not dependent on tips. Tipping the maître d' is not usually done except in situations where you get extra service. If she only shows you to your table, no tip is warranted.

Extra service from the maître d' can mean different things. If you're trying to avoid waiting for a table, want a particularly good table, or are requesting the maître d' to make special arrangements (for example, preparing the staff for a larger party or a special occasion or when you're entertaining clients) a tip may be offered. Ten dollars for a good table is fine. Offer more if you're trying to get a table at a busy time and wish to be seated before other waiting customers—try $20 to $25.

The timing of a tip to the maître d' depends on what you're trying to accomplish. If you need to get a table or would like a special table (such as one near a window or fireplace), tip him when making the request. If you've gotten the extra service you requested, or a

GIVING THE TIP

Here are a few guidelines to follow to make tipping easier:

▶ Have your tip money ready. Fumbling for cash in your pocket or purse will create an embarrassing and needlessly lengthy transaction.

▶ Look the person in the eye as you give them the tip. Making simple eye contact with the person who served you shows that you recognize them for the help they gave you.

▶ Thank them for the service. Expressing your gratitude makes it clear exactly why you're tipping—as recognition for a job well done.

special occasion went well, make your tip as you're leaving the restaurant. An appropriate way to do this is to deliver the tip while shaking hands and expressing your appreciation for a great evening.

Sommelier or Wine Steward

The sommelier or wine steward is often a part of the fine dining experience. He will have extensive knowledge of the wine list and be able to suggest wines that are complementary to your meal. He will also tend to the opening of your wine bottle, chilling or decanting if necessary, and pouring the first glass.

A tip for the services of the sommelier or wine steward can range from 10% to 20% of the price of the wine you choose. The lower amount is appropriate for the service of taking your order and pouring the first glass. If the sommelier is especially helpful in selecting the wine, is mindful of your budget, and returns to refill your glass, opt for the higher percentage. Take into consideration the cost of the wine and the number of bottles you've ordered. You may consider tipping at 10% to 15% when your wine bill is much higher than your food bill. If you're tipping the sommelier or wine steward separately, be sure to deduct the cost of the wine when figuring the tip for the waitstaff. There's no reason to tip on that amount twice.

Tip the sommelier when you're leaving. The sommelier usually will make himself available to you when you leave. Tip him directly in cash. If you need to add the tip to the credit card slip, be sure to let the headwaiter or captain know verbally or in writing what part of the tip is for the sommelier.

Captain or Headwaiter

The captain of the restaurant is in charge of the waiters and waitresses in one particular section of a large establishment. In a smaller restaurant, the headwaiter is in charge of the entire waitstaff. These servers usually share in the tips or the tip pool with the waiters and waitresses. The tip is generally split 25% to the captain or headwaiter and 75% to the waiter or waitress, who then tips the busperson from that money. Some finer restaurants may have a separate line item on the credit card charge slip for the captain or headwaiter. If this is available, separate the tip out. Otherwise, if you want to tip the captain or headwaiter for extra services, such as preparing sauces or dressings at the table, making special arrangements with the chef, or boning fish tableside, inform the server taking your payment about the percentage intended especially for the headwaiter or captain. These services warrant an extra 3% to 5% tip. You may also tip the captain or headwaiter in person with cash on your way out.

A NEW KIND OF CREDIT SLIP

Take a closer look at your credit card slip in a restaurant. You may be surprised to find a Gratuity Guideline at the bottom that gives you 15% or 20% gratuity amounts based on your individual bill. Although this is convenient, give these amounts a good looking over. You may find that these gratuity amounts are figured on the total *after* tax is added. If so, figure out the tip yourself and save a few bucks.

Doormen

Tips for doormen at restaurants can range anywhere from nothing to $5. If a doorman merely opens the door for you as you enter or exit, no tip is necessary. Performing special services warrants a tip. Some examples of special services and tip amounts are:

▶ Hailing a cab—$1.

▶ Hailing a cab in bad weather (rain or snow)—$2 to $5—depending on how hard the cab is to get.

▶ Carrying packages or a briefcase—$1 to $2.

▶ Carrying an umbrella over you in inclement weather—$2 to $3.

▶ Arranging to have your car at the door at a specified time—$2 to $3.

Hand the tip directly to the doorman when the service is performed.

Parking Valets

A parking valet takes your car from the front of the restaurant to a parking facility nearby. If the restaurant charges a fee for parking a car, no additional tip is necessary. If the restaurant does not charge a fee, the customary tip for a parking valet is $2 for getting your car, although $1 is acceptable. In larger cities, a tip of $2 to $3 is usual. If the valet takes the time to heat up or cool down your car, a $5 tip is generous but appropriate.

Washroom Attendants

These attendants are in charge of keeping the restroom facilities clean. If the restroom is clean, a tip of 25¢ to 50¢ is fine. Even if the attendant provides no extra service, a tip of at least 25¢ is nice. Handing you a towel after you're finished washing can warrant a tip of 50¢ to $1. In the unlikely, but welcome, event that the attendant helps you by brushing off your clothing or sewing on an emergency button, $2 to $3 is fine. If you find that you don't have any silver change on you, leaving a dollar bill will certainly be appreciated. Some swank clubs and restaurants supply an array of products for patrons to use, everything from perfume to breath mints, hair spray, and dental floss. When you use these free products, you may leave an extra 50¢ to

$1 for the attendant who keeps them orderly and replenishes them when necessary.

There is rarely a need to hand the tip to the attendant directly. There is usually a tray in a conspicuous place where you can drop your money.

Coat Check Attendants

Coat check areas are designed to keep your belongings safe and conveniently available to you. If the restaurant charges for this service, no tip is required. When there is no charge for this service, tipping 50¢ to $1 per garment is common. If you have extra packages, a briefcase, or a dripping umbrella, add an additional dollar. There is usually a basket available at the coat check window where you can leave your tip. If there isn't, hand the tip to the attendant when you turn in your coat check claim, or after you've collected all your belongings.

Entertainers

Some restaurants have musicians who perform for your enjoyment. Those that cater to families may provide a balloon artist or a magician to entertain children. While tipping these entertainers is not mandatory, it's not out of the ordinary either and will be welcomed by the performer.

Special requests to musicians are a prime example of a tipping opportunity. If a strolling musician stops by your table on her rounds about the restaurant, tipping isn't necessary, but it's perfectly appropriate if you've enjoyed the performance. If you request a tune, however, tip $1 per song. A large party with multiple requests can justify a $5 or $10 tip. Conversely, if you're in the middle of an important discussion and could do without the live sound track, feel free to wave away the musician, kindly—no need to tip. The proper way to tip the musician is to hand over the tip while expressing your thanks for the performance.

Treat a piano player in much the same way as a strolling musician. A tip is customary when you make a special request; $1 per request is fine. If you become the hit of the bar by singing all the tunes from *Oklahoma,* tip the piano player $5 to $10 for the fun. A basket or a large snifter is usually placed on the piano or very nearby for your tips.

Bands are mostly provided where there is dancing. If you make no special requests of the band, don't worry about a tip. If you do, $2 to $3 per request is nice since the band members split the tips. For larger bands, a tip of $5 or more for a special request is not unheard of. Give the tip directly to the bandleader, or give it to your server with the direction to pass it along to the band.

Entertainers in family or theme restaurants can be tipped the same way as musicians. The balloon artist or the magician will likely come to your table and perform for you. If you've been entertained, a dollar tip is a nice consideration. For a large party where the performer gives a balloon to each of the kids or a magician keeps the group enthralled for more than a minute or two, tip $2 to $5 depending on the special attention you've received. Give the tip directly to the performer with your thanks.

WHAT IF I HAVE A DISCOUNT COUPON OR A FREEBIE?

Just because you're paying less than full price (or nothing at all) for a meal doesn't relieve you of your obligation to tip the staff. You'll most likely be presented with a bill or an accounting of what your meal cost—along with an indication of the total bill *before* the discount was taken.

That's a hint. Base your tip on the amount your bill would have been if you'd paid full price. It's a fair expectation—the waiter did the same amount of work, whether you paid full price or not.

DIFFERENT **LOCALES**

Although more casual dining won't require as much money out of pocket for tips, tipping is still appropriate in the following situations.

Cafés and Coffeehouses

With the work required to make specialty coffees, a tip is a nice way to show thanks. Leaving a tip of 25¢ to 50¢ per order is adequate. Or leave the change you receive back from the server or the cashier—as long as it's more than a quarter. A tip jar or cup is usually provided at the counter.

In a sit-down café or coffeehouse where you have a server, a tip of 10% of the bill is fine. If you're ordering food also, you can up the tip to 15%. Even if you're just having a cup of coffee at the counter, leave a tip of $.25 or more. For drinks that require special preparation, or if you're getting refills, leave a bit more—$1 is more than adequate.

Buffets

Since the point of a buffet is to serve yourself, you may figure a tip is not necessary. The truth is that there are still servers there for you, and you should take them into account when paying the bill. A buffet server will usually take your drink order, keep your water glass full, clear your plate, serve coffee, and give you the check. A tip of 10% to 15% is sufficient for this service. If the server is especially attentive or offers to go into the kitchen to grab a piece of pie that wasn't on the buffet, tip on the higher end. Either leave the cash on the table or add their tip to the credit card slip.

NO TIPPING REQUIRED

There are a few people associated with your drinking and dining experience whom you shouldn't tip.

The owner of the establishment. Even if he or she greets you, seats you, and otherwise makes your experience pleasant, don't tip the owner. Instead, offer warm thanks as you leave and a promise to return.

The host or hostess. Like the maître d', the host or hostess handles your reservation over the telephone or takes your name at the desk if you are a walk-in, assigns your table and waiter, and may even walk you to your table and hand you your menu. But this service, although important, does not warrant a tip.

Anyone who treats you badly or disregards your requests. A rude car valet. A bartender who ignores you and makes you gesticulate wildly and beg for your drink. A coat check attendant who loses your satchel. In these situations, you have good grounds not to tip a farthing.

Cafeterias

Tipping in cafeterias is similar to buffet tipping. A 10% to 15% tip to the server is fine. If there is no service provided—you carry your own tray, get your own drinks, and clear your own place—no tip is necessary. Handing a tip to the busperson who clears the table is kind but isn't expected.

Tipping in Hotels

HOTEL ACCOMMODATIONS CAN RANGE FROM rooms in inexpensive budget chains to luxury suites in the finest hotels. As a rule, the more you pay for a room, the larger the number of people you will be tipping. Tips for restaurant and bar staff in hotels follow the same rules used for nonhotel establishments. The guidelines in this chapter will help you determine how much tips will add to your lodging costs.

LOBBY STAFF
Concierges

In French, the term *concierge* means "keeper of the keys." Your hotel concierge may not literally be keeping your keys, but she *is* the one with the information and the know-how to make your stay more pleasant and relaxed. A good one is above all resourceful and will attempt to help with any request, no matter how challenging. From getting theater or opera tickets to suggesting a nice lunch spot in the neighborhood, the concierge can do it. Some services don't warrant a tip; some do: booking a table at a restaurant; making arrangements for a private tour or a special excursion; getting tickets to the theater, the opera, or a sporting event; confirming or changing plane reservations; getting reservations at other hotels for friends who arrive unexpectedly when your hotel is full; arranging for a delivery, messenger, or fax service for business correspondence; renting a car; and arranging for baby-sitting.

How much to tip depends on what the concierge has done for you. For the services listed above, tipping between $2 and $5 is fine. Take into consideration how difficult it was for the concierge to obtain the help you needed. If you're looking for last-minute prime-time reservations to the trendiest restaurant in town or tickets to a sold-out art exhibit you've been dying to see, a tip of $10 to $20 is not inappropriate. For producing miracles—obtaining absolutely impossible-to-get tickets, such as floor seats to the Los Angeles Lakers during the playoffs or four seats together for *The Producers* on Broadway on a Saturday night—consider tipping 10% to 20% of the price of the tickets. It'll be costly, but if you're willing to pony up the money for the tickets, you should be prepared to pay for the effort it took to get them. Don't tip the concierge for simple things like directions to local shops, suggestions for lunch in the neighborhood, or brochures she has on hand. Nor need you tip the concierge if you haven't used her services at all during your stay.

You can certainly tip when the concierge provides the service—for instance, when she's handing you your tickets or as you're on your way out the door to the restaurant. Alternatively, if you use the concierge often, you may decide to tip her all at once at the end of your stay—especially if you've been dealing with her over the telephone and not in person. And if you know you're going to need some special services during your stay, it's a good idea to slip her between $10 and $20 as you check in. Introduce yourself and let her know you will need her assistance during your stay.

If you're tipping as you go or tipping before you even get any service, hand the concierge your tip with your thanks for her help. If you're uncomfortable handing her the cash directly, you may give it to her in an envelope. If you're tipping at the end of your stay, put the money in a sealed envelope with her name on it, and either give it to her directly or leave it with the front desk with instructions to forward it to her. When you've gotten the services of more than one concierge over the course of your stay, leave separate tips for each. If you don't know the name of the concierge who assisted you, check with the front desk and label the envelope appropriately.

A POCKETFUL OF ONES

Before heading off on a trip, be sure you have plenty of $1 bills in your pocket or handbag. Many people discover too late that the bills they're carrying are too large for the many small tips they need to make to doormen or bellhops, so they just don't tip at all. Come prepared with singles—up to $20 worth if you're flying and checking into a hotel—to make your tipping smooth and timely.

Doormen

Doormen are usually the first people you meet when you arrive at the hotel. They should be friendly, open your car door, and assist in unloading passengers and luggage at the front entrance. During your stay, they should also be willing to get you a taxi if you need one or to alert the valet service that you will need your car, if you haven't phoned the parking valet yourself.

The amount you tip a doorman depends on what service he provides. Upon arrival, if he just opens the door and signals for a bellhop, no tip is warranted. You may consider tipping him $1 or $2 if he helps you with your luggage or assists people in any way out of the car. During your stay, when the doorman gets a taxi for you, tip him $1 or $2, even if the taxi is waiting at the curb. Add an additional $1 to $2 if the weather is bad—rain or snow—and he shelters you under an umbrella while you get into the taxi. If you return to the hotel with a load of shopping bags and the doorman helps you get them out of the car, tip $1 for his help.

You should tip the doorman right after he performs the service—before you enter the car or taxi or as soon as you return to the hotel. If you are staying at the hotel for several days or longer, you may wish to tip the doorman in a lump sum, such as $10 to $15, either on arrival to guarantee good service or on departure to cover tips for your stay. If you tip on departure, be sure that you tip the doorman who has helped you most frequently, as the same doorman will not have been on duty around the clock. Introduce yourself when you give him the tip and thank him for the help he has provided during your stay.

Bellhops and Porters

Bellhops and porters are the people who transport your luggage to your room. They may even let you into your room, turn on the lights, and tell you about the amenities in your room and around the hotel.

How much you tip bellhops corresponds to the level of service provided, as with other hotel employees. Transporting your bags (whether carrying them or using a cart) warrants $1 or $2 per bag, with an additional $1 if the bags are very heavy. This applies both on arrival and on departure. If you are part of a large group, 50¢ per bag is okay if all the bags are carted together. If you're traveling with a tour group, a bag charge may be added to your hotel bill to cover the bellhop service. Ask your tour guide about this in advance; no tip is necessary if you're already paying for the service.

Reward extra assistance, such as turning on the lights, starting the heating or air conditioning, opening the curtains, and describing the hotel's amenities, with an extra $1 or $2. Delivery of newspapers, messages, faxes, packages, and complimentary fruit baskets warrant a $2 tip. If the bellhop goes to the drugstore (whether inside or outside the hotel) to get something for you, a $5 tip is fine.

Tip the bellhop at the time he provides the assistance. If you want to have an attentive bellhop at your service

O n a recent trip, I pulled up in front of my hotel and realized all I had in my wallet were a couple of $20s and a few $100s—not the kind of money I needed to tip all the people who would be helping me during the next 20 minutes. Instead of skipping the tips—as I had done before in similar situations—I decided to be direct with the doormen, the parking valet, and the bellhop. I asked each whether they could make change so that I could offer them a tip. I was pleasantly surprised to find they were happy to do so—the alternative for them, I guess, being no tip at all. When in doubt, ask.

TRAVEL LOG

—*Kelly G., Greensboro, North Carolina*

during your stay, offer a large initial tip, giving him the money when he brings your bags to your room. Let him know that you'll be looking forward to his help while you're staying at the hotel.

Parking Valets

Tip parking valets $1 or $2 each time they retrieve your car. If the garage is off hotel grounds, a $2 to $5 is good. If you'd like your car parked in the shade, or heated or cooled down before it's brought to you, or other special service, tip $5 or $10 the first time the valet takes your car, explaining your request clearly and offering thanks in advance. Careless handling may not warrant a tip, but be careful—no tip at all may bring wrath upon you and your car from the valet in the future. If your car has been treated inappropriately, alert the hotel management or the parking service at the same time you withhold your tip. There is no need to tip a parking booth attendant when you must retrieve your own car.

Tip valets when they bring the car around for you.

Maids

Depending on the type of hotel or the amenities offered, the level of service varies greatly. At any hotel you should expect at least a well-made bed, a clean room, trash removal, and fresh towels daily. Some hotels may also replace complimentary toiletries, clean and replenish the room coffee service, remove room service trays, and turn down your bed and leave a mint or a chocolate on your pillow every evening. In high-end hotels, rooms are freshened twice a day. The more service you receive, the greater the tip you should leave.

In an average hotel (with basic daily cleaning), tip between $1 and $3 per night—less in less expensive hotels, $2 or $3 in larger and more expensive hotels. If you've got a Jacuzzi or whirlpool room, or you've filled the room with kids who use every towel available and then leave them on the floor, you might leave up to $5 a night for the extra cleanup. For longer stays, $10 per guest per week is fine. If you've booked at a five-star hotel where the maids are in and out of the room more than once a day, a tip of $5 per night per guest is not unheard of. When you're paying big bucks for the room, you'll need to leave a bigger tip. There really isn't a need to leave a tip for a one-night stay, but $1 or $2 is considerate. If you'd like certain services, such as having the bed turned down at a specific time, the room cleaned early in the day, or extra towels and shampoo left in the bathroom, alert housekeeping and leave an extra $5 for the attention. In some hotels or if you're part of a tour group, a room-cleaning charge may be added. Ask the hotel or your tour guide in advance if there is a charge and whether the money goes to the housekeeping or cleaning people; no tip is required if you're paying this charge, but if you've left a particularly messy room, a tip is a nice gesture.

Many hotel maids leave a card or an envelope with their names on it for you to put a tip into. If an envelope is provided, you may leave a tip for the maid every day or you can leave one lump sum just before you check out. If there is no envelope in the room, you can leave the tip in a conspicuous place—say, on the pillow or on top of the desk—clearly marked so the maid doesn't think you left the money behind accidentally. If you're concerned about leaving the cash in your room, you may prefer to leave the tip at the front desk with instructions to give it to your maid. If you don't know her name, mark the envelope with your room number so the head of housekeeping can figure out who should get it. Or if you see your maid you can always hand the tip directly to her.

Making sure that the person who actually cleans your room gets your tip isn't always easy. Especially if you are staying for some time, different maids may service your room from one day to the next; in this case it may be more appropriate to tip every day. If you want to leave a lump sum, call housekeeping to get the names of the people who cleaned your room. Then you can leave an appropriate tip for each one. If you've received especially good service, don't hesitate to fill out the customer satisfaction questionnaire or the hotel comment card to report on the maid's excellent

WHAT ABOUT BED AND BREAKFASTS?

One of the charms of inns and B&Bs is the homey feel you get there. These hostelries are usually owner operated and owner occupied, so their home is your home. The proprietors are probably the waiters, bartenders, and housekeepers as well. For this reason, tipping isn't regularly done at B&Bs. A small gift or kind note ofthanks to the innkeepers is the best way to show your appreciation for their hospitality.

performance to hotel management. If service has been bad, alert the management as well—especially if you decide not to leave a tip at all.

Room Service Waiters

The duty of the room service waiter is to bring your food or drink order to your room. He may also set the table with linen and silver and open your wine. Tipping percentages for these services should be the same as for tipping waiters in a restaurant.

Tipping 15% of the total bill is customary for room service waiters. If the waiter ceremoniously opens the champagne bottle on your wedding night or sets a lovely table in front of a picture window, tip up to 20%. Tip at least $2 each time you receive room service—even if you're ordering only coffee.

The big issue in room service tipping arises when a room service charge or a gratuity is automatically added to the bill. Do you tip above and beyond these charges? The answer depends on the type of charge. Generally, a room service charge goes to the kitchen, and a gratuity (or a percentage of it) goes to the waiter. Even if a so-called gratuity is added to the bill, there still may be a line on the slip for an additional gratuity for the waiter. What to do? Simple—when placing your order, ask if there is a room service charge or a gratuity charge or both and find out to whom the money goes. If it's slated for the kitchen, go ahead and tip the waiter 15%. If the money is going to the waiter, you need not feel obliged to give an additional tip unless warranted by exceptional service.

Tip the waiter at the time of the service. When tipping in cash, hand it to him as he's departing. If you're adding it to your bill, fill in the gratuity amount on the slip when you're signing the bill.

OTHER SERVICE PROVIDERS
Excursion Guides

Expect to tip when you take an excursion—such as a canoeing or fishing trip, hiking or parasailing. If you ask the concierge to help arrange your outing, expect to tip him $3 to $5. Then plan to tip the folks who actually take you out on your adventure, commensurate with the price of the outing and, of course, with how much pleasure you got out of it. So, for example, plan to tip the captain and crew of your fishing excursion, or the pair of folks who take you out parasailing, or the guide who takes you on a private tour of the Uffizi. Between 10% and 20% is appropriate, depending on how elaborate the outing and how attentive the guide.

Tip in cash at the end of your excursion. If you're uncomfortable just handing over the bills, you may put your tip in an envelope.

We took an all-day fishing trip on our last vacation in Florida. The boat was big—maybe 35 guests, the captain, and 4 or 5 crew. We had a spectacular time; everyone in our party caught something respectable. The best part was the crew. They were always happily on hand to help you with bait or

TRAVEL LOG

removing your catch and were very encouraging to my 9-year-old son, who was having a little trouble catching a fish. When he finally did, they cheered and took his picture with his fish. Back at the dock at the end of the day, they presented each guest with his catch, all cleaned and filleted, no muss no fuss. Even though we paid plenty for the outing, I tipped the captain for a day that felt like it was spent among friends.

—*Maddy R., Galveston, Texas*

Room Assistants for Housekeeping or Repair

Whether you need an iron for your wrinkled shirt or an extra bottle of shampoo, the housekeeping department of your hotel can usually provide it. Those who assist you should be tipped for their service. As a rule of thumb, tip whenever a member of the hotel staff enters your room—even if it's just to adjust the temperature.

Tip the room assistant $1 to $2 per service. If you've requested multiple items to be brought at the same time, tip $1 per item for the extra work needed to gather the items before they're brought to your room.

Tip the room assistant in cash at the time of the service.

Take-Out Food Delivery

If your hotel doesn't have room service or you just have a hankering for a sandwich, a pizza, Chinese food, or a full meal from a restaurant outside the hotel, don't forget to tip the food delivery person. A good tip for the delivery person is 15% of the total food bill. Tip at least $1 or $2, even if you're ordering only a cup of coffee and a doughnut. Tip more if the weather is bad, if your order is large, or if the delivery person has to travel a long way to get to you. Ask for the total amount of your bill when you call in your order, so you'll know how much you're going to need to tip before the delivery arrives.

Tip the delivery person when she hands you the food. Give cash if you're paying in cash. If you're using a credit card, add the tip amount to the food portion of the bill and then total the bill so there's no mistake about the amount of the tip.

Hotel Shuttle Drivers

Whether you're taking a hotel shuttle to the airport or to area attractions, give the shuttle bus driver a tip. A typical tip is $1 per person and another $1 a bag for regularly scheduled runs. If you have to schlepp your own bags on board, $1 per person is fine. If you're on a special run of the bus—say, a 6 AM ride to the airport on a day when the regular schedule starts at 7 AM—tip $5 to $10 for the trip. For longer trips, tip another $1 or $2 per person. If the driver performs extra services, such as helping elderly people or people with disabilities in and out of the shuttle, tip an extra $1 or $2.

Tip the shuttle bus driver in cash at the end of the ride. If your ride is round-trip, tip the driver when you leave the shuttle at each end—you may have a different driver for each leg of the trip.

Valet and Shoe Polishing Services

Tip the valet between $1 and $5 for delivering your cleaning or pressing. A tip of $1 or $2 is fine for one or two items. For larger items or a whole rack of clothing, tip $5. If you're having your shoes polished, tip $1 or $2 for the service.

Tip the valet when your articles are returned. If you're not in your room at the time, don't worry about the tip. When leaving your shoes out for overnight polishing, tuck $1 or $2 in them by way of a tip. While leaving cash out in the hallway may be risky, you probably won't see the shoe service person, so this is the only way to deliver the gratuity. Tip both the valet and the shoeshine person in cash.

Tipping in Transit

THE SHUTTLE BUS DRIVER WHO MAKES SURE you get off at the right stop. The train porter who kindly moves your family to seats near the café car. The skycap who helps you bundle up your parcel so you can check it.

The people in the transportation industry are the ones who make sure you get where you're going. Tipping for their help is always appropriate, just as it is in restaurants and hotels.

AT THE AIRPORT

Skycaps and Luggage Porters

These people make sure your belongings go with you from the entrance of the airport terminal to the check-in counter or departure area. A skycap may check your luggage at curbside, for airlines and airports where curbside baggage check is available. Elsewhere, you may enlist the skycap or porter to cart your luggage from the curbside to the ticket counters inside the terminal.

Tip a skycap or porter at least $2 per bag, a little more if your luggage is heavy or unwieldy. Consider tipping up to $5 per bag during peak times or holidays, when things are usually very busy at the airport. If you or one of your party requires the use of an airport wheelchair, you may ask a skycap or porter to help push the chair. Tip $2 for this service. If he provides assistance in and out of the chair or is otherwise especially attentive, a $5 tip is appropriate.

Give the skycap or porter cash at the time of the service. If things are especially busy and you're in an incredible hurry, you may consider getting the skycap's attention by offering him an extra $5 or $10 over and above the standard tip to help you before others who are waiting. Do this by catching his attention with a wave of bills, or by quietly explaining your situation

NO TIPPING REQUIRED

While it's appropriate to tip some of the people who assist you while you're in transit, you don't have to tip everyone you encounter in getting from point A to point B. It's not appropriate to tip airline pilots, flight attendants, gate agents, baggage agents, or ticket agents. If you really want to express your gratitude to these individuals, by all means thank them personally or write a note to the airline commending their work.

to him while he is helping another passenger. Although this may offend or anger other people waiting in line, it could make the difference between catching your flight or missing it.

Taxi Line Attendants

In some cities, an attendant staffs the taxi area to make sure that passengers waiting for a taxi actually get one. She also keeps the taxi traffic running smoothly through the arrival area. If all she does is keep the line moving and direct you to the next available taxi, no tip is necessary. If she helps you with your bags, tip $1 or $2. Add an additional $1 or $2 if you have many bags or if they're heavy. Hand the taxi line attendant cash before you enter the taxi.

Cart Caddies

If you or your companion needs to be transported through the airport on a motorized cart, because of age or infirmity or the size of the airport, a cart caddy will drive you.

Tip the caddy $1 or $2 per passenger. If she's extremely pleasant and helps you with carry-on luggage or assists passengers out of the cart and to the gate, a tip of $5 is about right. Give her cash as you leave the cart or at the gate if she's helping you there.

ON THE ROAD
Cab Drivers

Often it's cabbies who are responsible for getting you where you're going in a new city. Ideally, you give them an address and they get you there. They pick you up, drive you to your destination, and let you out as close as possible to your stop as part of their basic service.

A tip of 15% to 20% of the fare is customary. If the driver helps you out of the car or collects your bags from the trunk, add an additional $1 per bag or an extra $1 or $2 for assisting you. If he's willing to make a stop and, say, wait for you at the drugstore, add an extra $1 or $2 for his trouble. You can also increase your tip if your cab driver points out local landmarks and tells you interesting anecdotes about them as he

On my first trip to New York, I discovered a category of car-for-hire called a "livery cab." It's not a yellow taxi and it's not a full-fledged limousine, but something in between. These cars are usually sedans, and though they aren't one color, make, or model, you can spot them by a nearly inconspicuous sign in the front window. Livery cabs don't have a meter or a set fee schedule, so—I learned—you have to be prepared to establish your price when you tell the driver your destination and before he starts driving you there. The price is likely to be all over the

TRAVEL LOG map—close to the price of a regular taxi ride or double or more what you'd pay for the same ride in a yellow cab, depending on the weather and the distance and how desperate you are to get where you're going in the absence of other available transportation. In my case, the driver proposed an exorbitant price for my ride downtown, I counterproposed, and we ended up somewhere in between. All this haggling before I'd even closed the car door—but, hey, it was raining hard and there hadn't been an unoccupied regular taxi in sight for 10 minutes. This is all by way of saying don't tip a livery cab driver—he's already tipped himself in his steep price for the ride.

—*Martin C., Boulder, Colorado*

ferries you through the city, or if he's driving you out of the way and has a slim chance of picking up a return fare. Also, tip him a bit extra if you'd like him to wait until you get inside the door at your destination—especially at night. Be sure to request this service before you get out of the car.

Tip in cash. Hand the money to him with your fare before you get out of the car, or hand it to him through the window after you exit the car. If he helps you out of the car or retrieves your bags, hand it to him curbside.

Tour Guides and Tour Bus Drivers

You will meet up with tour guides when you travel with a group in a privately hired bus or join a regularly scheduled tour around town. Either way, tipping the individuals who give you the tour may be appropriate.

Base tips for tour guides, the people who do most of the talking about the sights you visit, on their knowledge and enthusiasm. If you've had a good time and learned a lot, a tip is certainly appropriate. A dollar per person in your party for a tour of between two and four hours is fine. For excursions of a full day or longer, a tip of $1 or $2 per person per day is considerate. If the tour guide takes you on short walking tours during your trip, tip another $1 per person per day for the extra insight and for the effort it takes to keep track of the group. With tours that include overnight stays, tip the guide $3 or $4 per day. Private tour guides should be tipped between $2 and $10 per trip. Tip on the higher end for a full-day tour or for a larger party.

Sometimes the tour bus driver does all the talking about the destination. In these cases, tip the driver just as you would a tour guide. Again, your tip should reflect your appreciation of the tour. When a tour guide is also aboard the bus, you need not tip the driver separately for trips of a day or less. If you're out overnight or longer, a tip of $2 or $3 per person for the driver is fine. Tip a driver of a chartered bus without a guide between $20 and $30 for an overnight trip from the whole group. On longer charter trips, or if the driver is personable and adds an element of fun, an additional $10 or $20 or even more per day will signal your appreciation. If the price of the trip already includes tips for the tour guide and the driver, nothing additional is necessary.

When you are part of a trip organized for an affinity group, the group coordinator should organize the tipping. Usually a hat or a basket is passed around to gather the cash. On tours that you sign up for as an individual and on private tours, it's also appropriate to tip the guide or driver, in cash, yourself. Hand the money to them as you leave, and be sure to thank them for their time.

Limousine Drivers

Whether you've hired a private car with a driver to convey you around town or have booked a seat with a limousine service to shuttle you to the airport, it's de rigueur to tip the driver. Base your tip amount on the type of transportation you've chosen.

For airport limousine service, with a number of passengers transported to the airport in one vehicle, tip between 50¢ and $1 per person if it's crowded, $1 or $2 if there are fewer passengers. Add an extra $1 if the driver is exceptionally helpful with your luggage or with elderly passengers or travelers with a disability. If the cost of your limousine service is included in your airfare, no additional tip to the driver is necessary.

Private limousines transport only you and other members of your group, so a larger tip is appropriate—15% to 20% of the total charge. Opt for the higher percentage in larger cities. Many limousine services automatically add a 15%, 18%, or 20% gratuity to the cost of the service. You should be alerted up front, but if you're not sure, just ask. In this instance, no additional tip is necessary, although you can add an additional $5 or 5% if the driver is very helpful with your baggage or acts as an impromptu tour guide. This same rule applies to tipping a driver in a corporate car on a business trip. The gratuity should be charged to the company; any additional tip, perhaps $5 or $10, is up to you.

Most of the time it's appropriate to tip the driver in cash at the end of the trip—especially the driver of the airport limousine, when the amount of money is not large. For privately hired cars, tip in cash if you're tipping in addition to paying a gratuity charge. When you're tipping a percentage of the whole bill, you may either tip the driver in cash or ask for a specific tip to be added to your credit card slip or to your invoice if you're being billed for the service.

RIDING THE RAILS
Redcaps and Porters

The redcap or porter on a train will help you board, carry your luggage, and get you situated in your quarters on the train. Base your tip on the amount of luggage you have and the level of service you receive. A $2 or $3 tip is fine. If you have heavy luggage or a trunk, tip $5. Even if a service charge of 50¢ or $1 a bag is included in your fare, as is sometimes the case, an additional $1 or $2 is appropriate. On overnight or lengthy trips, the redcap or porter may help you again, delivering newspapers or bringing drink setups to your berth. For this additional service, tip up to $5 a night. If you don't see the redcap or porter again during a longer trip, no additional tip is necessary.

Tip the redcap or porter in cash—both upon arrival and departure—for helping with your bags. If he's been of assistance during the trip, you may tip him in cash when you receive the service or in a lump sum when you depart.

Dining or Club Car Waiters and Stewards

Whether you enjoy a leisurely lunch on a one-day train trip or take all of your meals in the club car when traveling for a week, you should tip the waiter and steward as you would in a restaurant.

The cost of your meals may be included in your ticket price—especially on longer trips. In this instance, the gratuity may be figured into the price of the meal. However, you may still tip the waiter $5 or $10 for particularly attentive service. On shorter trips during which you pay when you dine, tip the waiter 15% to 20% of the bill as you would in a restaurant.

A steward in charge of wine and drink service may also be aboard. Tip 15% to 20% of the wine bill. In addition to helping you choose a wine and serving it to you, he may also be in charge of delivering wine and drinks setups to sleeping cars and berths. Tip 15% to 20% of the price of the beverages.

Tip waiters and stewards in cash at the end of the meal if your meal is prepaid, since there will be no credit card slip to use for the tip. For other meals, you may either leave cash or write the tip on your credit card slip, just as you do in restaurants.

Sleeping Car Porters

Tip porters in sleeping cars on a per night basis. For service, which includes letting you into your car and setting up your sleeping berth, $2 per night per person is sufficient. Additional daily services you may request, such as making up the berth or wake-up calls, warrant a tip of $3 to $5 per night. Newspaper

---

Did you ever see Hitchcock's *North by Northwest?* I'm not referring to the famous cropduster scene, but rather the irresistible bit in the sleeping car on the train to Chicago. I decided to invest three days in a cross-country train trip so I'd get to ride in a sleeping

TRAVEL LOG car like Cary Grant and Eva Marie Saint. It was a memorable journey, made even more so because I accidentally locked my wallet in the overhead berth. The sleeping car porter helped liberate it, for which I gratefully tipped him a portion of its contents.

—*Elena V., Miami, Florida*

---

delivery or giving you advance notice of arrival at your destination should be tipped $1 or $2 per service.

Give the sleeping car porter your tip in cash when she provides the service. Alternatively, you can give the porter a lump sum in cash at the end of your journey for all daily services rendered during your trip.

Resort, Cruise, and Casino Tipping

RESORTS AND CRUISE SHIPS, WHERE YOU CAN TAKE
your pick of activities, personal services, and
entertainment, pose a comparably wide array
of tipping situations. The everyday dilemma
of whom to tip, when, and how much is com-
pounded in resorts and aboard cruise ships by
the different price structures—sometimes
your vacation is all-inclusive, with meals,
drinks, and entertainment included, and
sometimes you pay as you go. How you tip

varies from one situation to the next. Gambling destinations, increasingly popular across the United States, have their own unique set of tipping protocols, and it helps to be familiar with them before you venture out to the tables.

RESORTS

One of the draws of some resorts is the all-inclusive pricing package. This may or may not mean that tips are included, however. Some resorts truly are all-inclusive—the staff will not accept tips when they're offered. At other resorts, tips are accepted and expected. It is important to check with your travel agent or the resort to determine if your all-inclusive package means tips or no tips, and to whom exactly tips should be given. Filling out the customer comment card in praise of exceptional employees is always acceptable—whether or not a tip is expected or given.

Sports and Fitness

Golf

Golf instructors and caddies are considered essential personnel at many resorts. If you have a package, it may include greens fees and caddy fees; sessions with golf instructors usually entail additional fees. Tip a golf instructor $10 to $15 per day, or take yours to the clubhouse for drinks. If the instruction has helped you shave three strokes off your game, a bottle of good wine in addition to a tip is fitting.

Tip caddies per round—15% of usual caddy fees, if the fee has been included in the cost of your stay or your greens fees. When the caddy fees are not included and you have to negotiate the fees with the caddy yourself, tip between 15% and 50% of the fees you agreed upon, depending on how well she has worked for you.

Tip both instructor and caddy at the end of your game or session. If you're taking the golf instructor for drinks, arrange to meet when it's convenient for him. You may give him a bottle of wine or small gift before you leave the resort.

Tips should be in cash. Give the gratuity directly to the golf instructor or caddy along with your thanks, or leave the money at the pro shop's or resort's front desk in an envelope, clearly marked with the instructor's name and instructions that it be given to him when he's free.

Tennis

Although you don't usually tip a tennis instructor, you may invite her for drinks or dinner at your hotel if you feel you've been given excellent service. Or express your pleasure in a note of praise sent to the hotel management.

Skiing

Ski instructors are not usually tipped. If you'd like, you can invite the instructor for drinks or dinner as an expression of your appreciation. Do not tip pro-shop employees either, although if someone digs up the last pair of size eight boots on a holiday weekend, you may wish to hand over $5 in recognition of your appreciation for the determination it took to find them for you. This is the exception, not the rule, however.

Fitness centers

Whether you tip the trainers in a hotel fitness center depends on the type of service you receive. If you're working out and a trainer comes over to help you adjust a machine or give you advice on how many reps to do, no tip is necessary. On the other hand, if you schedule a private session with a personal trainer, a tip is in order; 15% to 20% of the cost of the session is appropriate.

You may tip locker room attendants $5 a day if your service has been great. If they have brought you robes, towels, beverages, or personal care items, this kind of tip is warranted. Regular staff members of a fitness center, such as the front desk personnel and class instructors, don't receive tips.

Tip personal trainers before you leave for the day. Because you probably won't have a $20 bill tucked into your sock during your session with the personal trainer, leave your tip in an envelope marked with the trainer's name at the front desk of the fitness facility. Envelopes will probably be available for just this purpose. You may include a personal note of thanks if you wish.

Tip locker room attendants before you leave the locker room, in cash. If you see the person who helped you before you leave the locker room, deliver the tip directly. If not, leave it in an envelope at the center's front desk with instructions to pass it along to the attendant.

Water sports

When you're participating in water sports where you've been instructed or taken on an outing, tipping is appropriate. Expect to tip whoever has been with you during your activity: the guide on your canoe trip; the instructors at the waterfront; the people who help you get on your way when you go out jet skiing, surfing, sailing, windsurfing, parasailing, kayaking, or snorkeling; and the captain and crew on a fishing boat, whether or not they help you land the big one.

Use your judgment when tipping these people. Base your tip on how attentive they were to your needs and how much you enjoyed your experience. Your canoe guide can be tipped $5 to $10 for making your canoe trip great. Instructors and other key people in charge of your water sports should be tipped between $5 and $10 per session. Tip the captain and crew of a fishing party boat about $20 for their help. If you've chartered a boat for fishing, tip the captain 15% to 20% for his work and the crew's.

Personal Care

Masseuses and Masseurs

Gratuities for a masseuse or masseur are always a percentage of the charge for the massage—15% to 20% of the price, up to 25% if the massage is in your room. If a 15% or 20% gratuity charge is added to your bill, as occasionally happens, you may add a little extra, between $5 and $10. Ask whether the gratuity will be included in your charge when you book the treatment.

Tip before you leave the spa or after the massage is completed. You may pay in cash or charge the tip along with the fee for services to your credit card or to your room. For cash tips, spas often provide envelopes. Be sure to mark your envelope with not only the masseuse or masseur's name but also your own (or your room number). When charging the tip to your credit card or to your room, add the gratuity to the tip line on the charge slip and total the charges.

Hair stylists and barbers

Tip a hair stylist 15% to 20% of the price of the service. Of course, if you walk in looking as if you've just been through a hurricane and come out looking like Julia Roberts, tip the 20% and slip in an extra $10. The

My husband surprised me on my 40th birthday with a gift of five days by myself at a health spa in the Berkshires. I had never done that sort of thing, so I was overwhelmed (and delighted) by the sports and personal care that were part of my package. And I did it all—massages, facials, kayak lessons, swim classes, a personal Pilates session, yoga three times a day—you name it. I thought I had died and gone to heaven. I had an idea of how expensive my stay was and, because it was called a "package," I naively assumed that all expenses were covered.

TRAVEL LOG

Weeks later it dawned on me that perhaps I should have tipped all the nice housekeepers, waiters, and health, grooming, and fitness professionals who had so professionally tended to me. When I called the spa to inquire as to tipping customs, I was mortified to discover that, indeed, tips are appreciated by one and all. With the help of one of the program coordinators, I was able to identify most of the people who had assisted me during my stay and then I sheepishly sent along gratuities after the fact. Better late than never. Even better, figure it out in advance.

—*Karyn R., Red Hook, New York*

shampoo person should get $2 to $5 as well. Barbers should get 15% to 20% of the charge.

Tip all of these people at the conclusion of your service. Tip the hair stylist and the barber in cash if paying cash, or add the tip to your bill or your credit card charge slip. The shampoo person should be tipped in cash.

Manicurists

Tip a manicurist 20% of your charge. If she's squeezed you in, add another $1 or $2 for her trouble. Some spas make the gratuity part of the fee for a manicure or pedicure; ask the receptionist about this when you book. If the tip is included, nothing extra is necessary unless you're very happy with the service—if you are, you may want to tip an extra $5 above the gratuity charge.

Give the manicurist the money at the end of the treatment. If you are paying cash, tip in cash. Otherwise, write in the tip on your credit card charge slip or on your room bill.

At the Pool and on the Beach

Lifeguards

Lifeguards are not usually tipped, either at the pool or the beach. If one of them saves you or a member of your family from drowning, thank him or her profusely—but don't offer a tip.

Towel booth staff

When a person behind a counter hands you a towel, no tip is required. If, on the other hand, someone brings fresh towels to your spot on the beach or beside the pool, tip $1 or $2 for the extra attention.

Tip the towel booth attendant in cash at the time of the service.

Waiters and waitresses

When a waiter or waitress brings you beverages and snacks at the pool or on the beach, tip 15% of the bill, at least 25¢ or 50¢ for smaller orders. You can tip up to 20% if it's a devilishly hot day and the server has to cross a desert of burning sand to deliver your order.

Tip when you receive your food or at the end of your time at the pool or beach if you're running a tab. If paying with cash, tip in cash. If you are charging your bill to a credit card or to your room, add the tip to the charge slip and total the bill.

Chair or cabana staff

Setting up your chair or opening up your cabana for the day warrants a $1 or $2 tip. Additional services such as delivering extra chairs or towels justify another $1 or $2. Add a $1 or $2 ($5 isn't unheard of) if the staffer helps you lug loads of gear to your spot.

Tip the cabana or chair staff in cash at the time of the service.

Other Services

Laundry

Laundry personnel and valets should be tipped as they would be in a regular hotel. Tip $1 to $5 for delivering your cleaning or pressing. For larger orders, tip $5.

Tip when your articles are returned. Tip in cash or charge the tip to your house charge. If you're not around when your items are delivered, don't worry about a tip.

Child care

When a baby-sitter takes care of your children in your room or suite and all goes smoothly, tip $5 per session. If your kids are all smiles and full of happy tales when you come back, you can signal your appreciation by tipping even more. When you can leave your offspring with a bunch of other children for an afternoon at a re-sort child care center, a tip to the staff is not necessary.

Tip the baby-sitter in cash when she leaves your room. If you've had a particularly wonderful experience, consider dropping a note to the resort management.

CRUISES

Tipping is one of the biggest question marks about cruising, and even frequent cruisers often need guidance. While you may call at different ports, most of your activities for a number of days are aboard the ship, and you encounter many of the same service people day in and day out. So, rather than tipping repeatedly at the time of service, you may distribute tips at the end of a voyage or, alternatively, hand them out at intervals during the trip; significant tips, given at the end of a 7- to 10-day trip, might be offered weekly during a longer voyage, for instance.

Some cruise lines publish tipping guidelines, so that you can plan your tips—and accurately calculate your travel expenses—before you board the ship. Envelopes are usually provided specifically for tipping the cruise personnel. Other cruise lines discourage tipping altogether. It's essential to ask your cruise line or your travel agent for tipping guidelines at the time you book your journey to be sure you have enough cash or traveler's checks at the end of the voyage for your tips.

In the Dining Room

You will be assigned a table in the main dining room for the length of your cruise and the same waitstaff will attend to your needs day after day. Tips are figured per day per person.

Waiters and waitresses

Tip your waiter $3 or $4 per person per day. Do you include a tip for nights you do not eat in the main dining room—say, when you elect to dine in a specialty restaurant or go for a buffet? You can, but it's not obligatory. Some cruisers err on the side of generosity and include the extra in the total amount. Others tip only for days they actually ate in the main dining room. Either way, the size of your tip within the range should reflect the quality of the service you receive. When dining at the reservations-only specialty restaurants, leave a tip of $5 per person. Tipping is not customary at buffets.

Tip your waiter on your last night out on a voyage of 10 days or less. On a longer cruise, tip the waiter once a week—usually on Friday night—so he or she will have some money to spend when the ship docks at different ports.

Give the waiter your tip in cash. If for some reason you can't tip your waiter in person, you can leave the tip in an envelope with the purser's office before you depart. Mark the envelope with the name of your waiter, along with your name and table number if you have it. If you changed tables during the cruise, tip each waiter who served you separately for the time they served you. Tip the waiter in a specialty restaurant in cash after you've finished your meal.

Buspeople and waiter assistants

The buspeople or waiter assistants are the second part of your waitstaff team that you should recognize with tips, usually $1.50 or $2 per person per day. If you're tipping the waiter for evenings that you don't eat in the main dining room, tip the busperson and assistant, too. The waitstaff and buspeople or assistants work as a team and should be tipped in tandem.

Tip the busperson or waiter assistant the last night of your cruise for a shorter trip, weekly (on Friday night) for longer voyages. Deliver your tip in cash at the end of the meal. If you can't find your busperson or assistant, you can leave the tip with your waiter with directions to pass it along. If you must leave the tip with the purser's office before disembarking, be sure to mark the envelope with the busperson's or waiter assistant's name.

Headwaiters

Headwaiters in a cruise ship's dining room, as in a restaurant, are in charge of sections of the dining room. Tip $2 per day per person. If a special service is provided, a higher amount is appropriate. If you've had no contact with the headwaiter, there's no need to tip.

Maître d's

The maître d' is there to be sure the dining room runs well. She's the one to see if you're not happy with your table assignment or if you want to arrange a special birthday or anniversary celebration. A tip of $1 or $2 per guest per day is appropriate. If she arranged a party for you or worked hard to find you a suitable table, definitely tip on the higher side with perhaps an additional $10 to $20 for the extra attention. If you've seen the maître d' only when you were first seated in the dining room and in passing as she made her way around the dining room during the cruise, tip on the lower end of the scale or perhaps not at all.

The maître d' should receive her tip on the last evening of a shorter cruise and weekly, preferably on Friday nights, if your journey lasts longer than 10 days. Tip her in cash after dinner or leave the tip in an envelope marked with her name at the purser's office before you disembark.

Wine stewards

Wine selections are rarely included in the cost of your cruise. Because you are charged separately for your wine, you can tip the wine steward a percentage of your bill as you would in a restaurant. Between 10% and 15% is appropriate—more if she's been particularly helpful. Some cruise lines advise passengers to tip the wine steward daily— $1.50 per guest per day on the evenings you have wine.

Tip the wine steward when you are presented with your bill at the end of the meal. If you're tipping based on a daily per person guideline, do so the last evening of the cruise or weekly for longer trips.

When presented with the bill, you may tip the wine steward in cash then and there. Or you can add your gratuity to the bill, which will be added to your shipboard account, to be settled up at the end of the voyage. When tipping a set daily amount, tip in cash. If you don't see the wine steward the last evening of your cruise, you may drop off the tip in a marked envelope at the purser's office before leaving the ship.

Bartenders

Alcoholic beverages are not usually included in the price of your cruise. Bar tabs are often charged to your shipboard account, which is settled at the end of the trip. For simplicity's sake, most cruise lines automatically add a 15% gratuity to all bar bills. Ask your travel agent or the cruise line about the policy aboard your ship before you sail. If a gratuity is not included, tip the bartender 15%.

The time to tip is before you leave the bar. You may do so in cash or add the gratuity onto your bill.

NO TIPPING REQUIRED

On a cruise ship, you do not tip the captain, any ship's officer, or the cruise director. Instead of giving them gratuities, you may graciously thank them each in person for their part in making your trip enjoyable. You can also drop a note to the cruise line lauding any particularly excellent service you received.

In the Cabin

Cabin stewards

The steward is in charge of your needs in the cabin, from keeping it tidy to bringing extra towels. Figure the tip on a daily basis, reflecting the service you receive; $3 to $4 per guest per day is fair. When the steward performs little extras, such as giving you a wake-up call or turning down your bed, tip at the higher end of the range. If you're occupying the top cabin aboard a luxury ship, tip up to $5 per guest per day. In the unlikely event your treatment is rotten, you have the option not to tip at the end of your trip. If you do this, be sure you let the purser and the steward know why.

Tip the cabin steward on the last evening of your cruise. For voyages of longer than 10 days, tip the steward weekly on Friday nights. When tipping in advance, tip in cash. When tipping at the end, some cruisers rely on traveler's checks for tipping larger amounts, although cash is always appropriate. Leave your tip in an envelope on the dresser or somewhere else obvious with the steward's name on it. If you'd like, you can leave the tip in the purser's office on the day you disembark. In either case, a personal note of thanks to the cabin steward included with the tip is a nice gesture.

Butlers

Butlers are usually available only for travelers who book suites on a cruise. They're in charge of fewer rooms than cabin stewards, so the service is more personal. If you've got a butler, tip him $5 per guest per day.

Tip the butler at the end of the trip, on the evening before you depart. On longer cruises, you may tip weekly, usually on Friday nights. Tip in cash—leave the money in an envelope in your suite with the butler's name on it, or give the envelope to the purser's office. Here, too, a personal note of thanks is gracious and appropriate.

Room service personnel

Tip the waiter who brings you a room service order $2. If you've gone all out and ordered a meal fit for a king, up the tip to $5 or more for the trouble of bringing everything and setting it up in your cabin.

Tip the room service waiter when you receive the order. Give cash or add the gratuity to the bill to be charged to your shipboard account.

Personal services

Hairdressers, manicurists, barbers, and masseuses should all be tipped as they would be on land; 15% to 20% of the cost of the service is appropriate.

Tip for personal services at the end of the appointment. You may offer cash or add the gratuity to the bill.

Dock porters

Tip dock porters like skycaps or redcaps—$2 per bag for regular-size luggage with an additional $1 or $2 for trunks. The heavier the bag, the greater the tip should be.

Tip the porter in cash when he renders the service.

Entertainment and Activities

Deck stewards

When deck stewards bring you drinks by the pool or on deck, tip 10% to 15% of the tab. For bringing you a pack of gum, a newspaper, or a blanket, or for doing other favors, offer $1 per task at the time of service. Render smaller tips in cash, although it's okay to add larger gratuities to your bill.

Excursion planners

Excursion planners who are employed by the cruise line and act as tour guides at ports of call should be tipped $5 per person. Use your judgment—if you had a fabulous time, tip more. Tip in cash as you return to the ship.

was delighted by the bright, attentive stewards who gave us truly four-star poolside deck service on a Caribbean cruise. On the last day, I inadvertently left my very expensive French suntan lotion behind, and when I rushed back to the pool an hour later it was gone. But no! At the steward's station, I discovered

TRAVEL LOG

my lotion on the counter, marked neatly by my steward with my name and ready to be delivered to my cabin. Needless to say, I hunted down the steward and thanked (and tipped) him enthusiastically. The lotion I certainly could have lived without—but his kindness and conscientiousness were above and beyond.

—*Lisa D., Stewart, Virginia*

Activity coordinators, photographers, musicians, and performers

These people on board ship are usually not tipped (an exception being a piano player at a bar, who should be tipped as at any bar on land). If service has been outstanding, however, a tip isn't inappropriate.

CASINOS

At the Tables

There are more games in casinos than you can shake a stick at, and each has its own tipping protocol. The guidelines below give you an idea of what to expect; when playing other games not mentioned here, you can follow the same general rules—and ask the dealer or the pit boss for guidance on tipping etiquette if you're really stuck.

The key thing to remember is that tipping at the tables depends on whether you're winning or losing. If you're winning, it's expected that you'll share the wealth with the dealer who helped make it happen. If you're in the red, nobody wants you to torture yourself worrying about tips. Tipping as you go along instead of at the end of your time at the table enables you to deal appropriately with all the vicissitudes of a typical session.

Playing the Games

Blackjack dealers

The amount you tip blackjack dealers depends on how much you bet and how successful you are. A $1 or $5 chip given to the dealer when you win a hand or two is fine. If you're into betting big bucks, tip $10 to $25 while you're playing and more if you hit a jackpot. What about when you hit the big one? Although the dealer has no control over what cards you receive, she should still be tipped well when you win big—5% to 10% is appropriate. If you're feeling generous and have won enough to pay off your house, tip 10% or more. A tip of between $5 and $20 for your whole time at the table when you've won a few and lost a few is also acceptable.

Tip a blackjack dealer either while you're playing or at the end of your time at the table, or both. Since dealers don't often stay in one place for a long period, tipping while you play insures that the dealer who's in charge of the table while you're winning will get a tip.

There are a couple of ways to convey the tip. You can push a chip toward the dealer (dealers are rarely tipped in cash); she'll tap it on the table before depositing it into her tip box. You can also place a side bet for the dealer—usually about half of your own bet. Place the chips you wish to bet outside the circle and announce that this bet is for the dealer. If you win the hand, the side bet goes to the dealer. If you lose, well, that's the way it goes.

Poker dealers

Poker players usually tip dealers during the course of a session. Take a chip or two out of the pot when you win a hand. A big winning hand could garner 5% to 10% or more for the dealer. You can always tip $5 to

$10 at the end of your session of play if you want to tip all at once.

Tip the dealer either when you win a hand or at the end of your session at the table. Tipping as you go insures that the dealer at the table while you're winning will get the tip.

Tip the poker dealer in chips of whatever denomination you choose while you're playing. If you win big, you can tip the dealer in cash after you've settled your winnings with the casino.

Craps dealers

You tip craps dealers the same way you tip other table dealers. During play, tip the dealer $10 or $20 for a good roll. You can also place a bet for the dealer while you're playing by placing the chips next to your own bet and announcing the bet is for the dealer. "Betting for the boys" is common, as the dealers like to be in on the action with you. You may also leave a $5 to $10 tip at the end of the session if you haven't tipped while you played. If you're tipping for a good roll, put down your chips while collecting your winnings from the dealer.

Keno runners

Keno is a casino game that resembles a lottery. So-called runners take the ticket with your number selections to the clerk, return with your duplicate ticket, and find you to deliver your winnings if you're outside the Keno area. Tip $1 for the first run, and an additional $1 or $2 from time to time as you play—even if you're losing. A 10% to 15% tip is appropriate if you hit big.

Around the Casino

Cocktail waiters and waitresses

While drinks are usually free while you're playing, the hard-working cocktail servers should be tipped at least $1 per round. If you're up some money at the table, a $5 tip is a fitting way to share your success.

Tip the server when she brings your drink. You may tip in cash or with a chip.

Change clerks and slot attendants

Tip change clerks and slot attendants $1 or $2 when they respond to your call for service or answer questions. If the attendant gives you advice about which machine is hitting big, and it does, tip 10% or more of your jackpot. Give a tip of 5% to 10% to the attendant who comes to make the cash payoff after a big win.

Tip change clerks when they come to make change. Tip slot attendants when they service a machine, fill the hopper, or attend to the machine when you win a big jackpot. You can tip in cash (as most machines use real money these days) or with a chip if you have one. If you get a big payoff, you'll get some of your winnings in coins and the rest in "folding money," which you can also use for the tip.

Bartenders

Tip the bartender $1 or $2 per round for a party of one to four people. If your party is larger, tip up to $5 per round. If you're having an especially good time and the bartender is helping make that happen, drop him another $5 to $10 when you leave.

The bartender should be tipped when you receive your drinks. When you're running a tab, tip when you pay the bill. Tip him in cash or with chips, or add the gratuity to the charge slip if you're paying with a credit card.

Parking valets

Tip the valet $1 or $2 every time your vehicle is brought to you. If you'd like the valet to keep an eye on your car, give him $5 or $10 when you hand over the keys and make your request. Either way, the tip should be in cash.

Washroom attendants

If the washroom is kept tidy, or if the attendant hands you a towel or directs you to a stall when it becomes free, tip the attendant 25¢ or 50¢ or even $1. There's usually a tray or basket on the counter, and a chip is as appropriate as cash.

5

International Tipping

WHEN YOU TRAVEL OUTSIDE THE UNITED STATES, there's a whole wide world of service people you'll have dealings with. While the practice of tipping crosses most borders, standards for how much to tip and when to do so vary from country to country. Familiarizing yourself with these standards before setting out on your trip makes it easier and less intimidating to tip the right amount at the right time—or not, if nothing is expected.

To help you zero in on the information you need, we've organized the following worldwide overview of basic tipping practices by region and alphabetically by country. The list of countries and tipping scenarios, although not comprehensive, should stand you in good stead for the circumstances you'll encounter most frequently on the road.

EUROPE

Andorra

Restaurants often add a 10% to 15% service charge to the bill, but it is customary to leave a matching amount as a tip for the waiter. Taxi drivers should get 10% of the fare as a tip. Hotels will apply service charges directly to the bill so no additional tips are necessary.

Austria

In restaurants a 10% service charge is usually added to the bill. If you'd like, you can tip an additional 5% for exceptional service. Hand the tip directly to the waiter. Tip taxi drivers 10% of the fare. Tip hotel porters €1 per bag and chambermaids €1 per day.

Belgium

If no service charge has been added to the bill, it's common to tip 10% in restaurants. If a service charge is included and the service is good, tip by rounding up the payment to the nearest euro. A tip is usually included in the cost of a taxi ride, so nothing extra is necessary, although, for good service, you may round up the fare as a tip for the driver. Porters and hotel help customarily receive €1 per service.

Bulgaria

Tip both waiters and taxi drivers 10% of the bill. Bellhops are normally tipped the equivalent of US$1 per service. Tip hotel staff 10% to 20% at expensive hotels, 10% at smaller establishments.

Cyprus

Hotels and restaurants add a service charge of 10% to all bills. Add 5% for exceptionally good service in restaurants. Small change is always appreciated by taxi drivers and hotel porters. Tip the equivalent of US$1 to each.

Czech Republic

In restaurants if the gratuity is not already included in a service charge, a tip of 10% is appropriate. If you'd like, round up the bill to the nearest multiple of 10 or add an extra 5% to bring the tip to 15%. Hand the waiter the money for the bill and the tip directly—don't leave it on the table. Give taxi drivers 10%. In better hotels tip the doorman and the bellhop who help you with your luggage 10Kc (10 korunas) to 20Kc.

Denmark

Tipping in Denmark is not customary because prices generally included gratuities. For superior service, you may give an additional 5% to 10%. Hotel porters receive about kr1 (1 krone) per bag.

Estonia

Restaurants sometimes add a 10% service charge. You can tip an extra 10% for exceptional service. If your bill does not include a service charge, a 15% tip is standard. Service charges are included in hotel bills, but small tips are always appreciated. Tip taxi drivers 10% to 15% of the fare.

Finland

Prices in restaurants ordinarily include service charges. You can leave a few extra euros for very good service. In hotels give a €1 or €2 to the bellhop who brings your bags to your room (not to the doorman). Round up the fare to the nearest euro as a tip for the taxi driver. Train or hotel porters also receive €1 for a tip.

France

The French word for tip, *pourboire* means "for a drink"—tips are supposed to be "for drinking money" or, in other words, pocket money. Restaurant and bar bills usually include a service charge, but a tip of €1.50 is appreciated. Tip taxi drivers 10% of the fare. Give coat check attendants €.30 to €.75 unless it's posted "Pourboire Interdit," forbidding tipping. Offer restroom attendants €.30 as you leave. In hotels, tip baggage porters €1.50 per item, chambermaids €1.50 per day if you have stayed two or three days or more. Room service waiters should be tipped €1.50 when they deliver the food. Give tour guides €1.50 per day; another €1.50 to the bus driver. Tip museum tour guides €.75 to €1.50. Ushers in movie theaters should be tipped €.15 or €.30. Tip museum guides €.75 to €1.50 after a guided tour. Do not tip gas station attendants for just pumping gas or checking your oil, but tip €.75 to €1.50 for checking the tires. Train and airport porters should be tipped €.90 to €1.50 per bag.

Germany

Restaurant bills generally include a service charge. Rounding up the bill to the next euro or so is an appropriate tip beyond the service charge. Leaving the tip on the table is considered rude, so hand it directly to the waiter. Tip taxi drivers by rounding up to the next €1 or €2 from the cost of the fare. Offer airport and rail porters €1 or €2 above the price of the service. In hotels, tip the porter €1 per bag. Maids should be tipped €4 a day in luxury hotels, €2 a day in other hostelries. Tip room service staff at least €2 each time you order.

Great Britain

Most restaurants add a 10% to 15% service charge to your bill, and no other tip is necessary. If a restaurant hasn't, tip 10% to 15%. Don't tip the bartender in a pub. Offer taxi drivers 10% to 15% of the fare. Give porters and hotel help a tip of £1 (1 pound) per service, maids £1 per person per day. If you use the services of the hotel concierge, a £1 to £2 tip is appropriate. Tip washroom attendants 20p (20 pence) to 50p when you leave. You don't need to tip theater or cinema ushers.

Greece

In Greece a service charge is figured into all meal prices but round the bill up to an extra 10% by way of a tip. Tip hotel porters €.60 per bag and maids €.60 per day. When taking a taxi, tip the driver by rounding the fare price up to the nearest €.30. Theater and cinema ushers should be tipped €.60 and €.30 respectively when you take a program.

Hungary

In restaurants tip 10% to 15% of the bill. Pay the waiter directly—don't leave the tip on the table. Gypsy bands playing in restaurants should be tipped 200Ft (200 forints) for the entertainment. Give the tip to the bandleader as the band leaves your table. Taxi drivers normally are tipped 10% to 15% of the fare. Offer hotel porters 100Ft per service.

Iceland

Tipping is not customary in Iceland.

Ireland

If a 12% service charge has been added to the restaurant bill, no additional tip is necessary, unless you'd like to reward excellent service with an additional 5% tip. If no charge has been added, tip at least 10% of the bill. It's not customary to tip barmen in pubs, but you should tip waiters in bars and hotel lounges or Dublin lounge bars about €7.65. For most taxi rides, tip the driver 10% of the fare. For longer trips, where you've negotiated the price with the driver, no additional tip is necessary. Tip hotel porters €.65 per bag; tip €1.30 per bag in luxury hotels.

Italy

In major cities it is customary to add a 5% to 10% tip to the restaurant bill, even though it usually includes a service charge. In hotels a service charge is added to your hotel bill, but you can give a small amount to hotel staff as tips—€.75 per day to maids, €.50 to €1 per service to bellhops, at least €.50 per service for room service waiters and housekeeping valets, and €.25 for a doorman who calls you a cab. If the concierge has been especially helpful, tip him up to 15% of his bill. Give taxi drivers 5% to 10% of the fare. Offer tour guides €1 per person for a half-day group tour and more if you're very pleased.

Latvia

Restaurant bills normally include a service charge, but it is customary to add a tip of 5% to 10%. No additional tip is necessary unless you receive excellent service. If no service charge is added, add a 10% tip to the bill total. Taxi fares may include a tip, but if not, tip 10% of the metered fare.

Lithuania

A service charge is usually added to restaurant bills. While no additional tip is necessary, a 10% tip for excellent service is appreciated. Taxi fares include the tip, but you may round up the bill. Porters receive 2Lt (2 litai) per bag. No extra tip is expected in hotels since the price includes a service charge.

Luxembourg

At hotels and restaurants you can give a small tip in addition to the service charges added to the bill. Round up to the nearest €2.50 when paying the bill. Porters, bellhops, and doormen can be tipped €1.25 to €1.50 per service. Taxi drivers expect a tip of 15% of the metered fare.

Malta

When a service charge is not added to the bill in a restaurant or hotel, tip 10% of the bill. Tip taxi drivers 10% of the fare. Tip porters the equivalent of US25¢ per bag. Tip maids the equivalent of US50¢ per week. This seems like very little, but hotels customarily include a 10% to 15% tip in the bill.

Netherlands

Hotels and restaurants almost always include a service charge in their bill, and no additional tip is necessary. You may round up the bill if the service was particularly good. Tip bellhops in first-class hotels €.90 for each bag. Coat check people should be tipped at least €.50 per service. Taxi meter charges include a tip, but you can round up the fare for the driver. Doormen get a tip of €1 to €1.50 for calling a cab.

Norway

A service charge is usually included in hotel and restaurant bills. There's no need for an additional tip, though you can add 5% to 10% for exceptional service. Tip taxi drivers if they've been helpful with the luggage—just round up the fare to the next round digit or tip from kr5 (5 kroner) to kr10 or more if the driver has been especially helpful. A porter should be tipped kr15 to kr20 for helping with your luggage.

Poland

Giving a 10% tip to the waiter is customary when no service charge has been added to the bill. Otherwise, round the bill up zl1 (1 zloty) to zl2 for good service. Tip porters and hotel doormen zl2 per bag. Taxi drivers should receive a 10% tip.

Portugal

Most restaurant and hotel bills include a service charge. Give a few extra coins in change to the waiter for good service. Hotel porters should be tipped €1 per service, while maids should be tipped €1 per day. Tip taxi drivers 10% of the fare. Tip train and airport porters €.50 per bag.

Romania

Romanians themselves don't tip, but in restaurants a tip of 10% to 12% is expected of foreigners. Give the tip to the waiter or cashier—don't leave it on the table. Tip taxi drivers 5% to 10% of the fare. Hotel bellhops should be tipped US$1 to US$2. Tip airport and train station porters US$2 for a few bags. Tips in U.S. dollars are accepted everywhere.

Russia

Tipping is now the accepted norm in Russia. Cloakroom attendants, waiters, porters, and taxi drivers will all expect a tip. A 10% gratuity is generally incorporated in restaurant bills, but you can tip an additional 5% for good service. If no service charge has been added, tip 10% to 15% of the bill. When paying by credit card, leave the tip in cash as it's easy to miss the tip on a credit card slip. Add a tip of 10% of the fare for a taxi driver. In luxury hotels in Moscow and St. Petersburg, tip the doorman who helps you with your bags 100 rubles.

Scotland

If no service charge is added to the restaurant bill, tip the waiter 10%. If there is a service charge, no additional tip is expected. Bartenders in pubs are not tipped. Tip taxi drivers 10% of the fare. Tip hotel porters £1 per bag.

Slovakia

For good service in a restaurant, tip 10% if a service charge has not been added to the bill and an additional 5% in restaurants when the check includes the gratuity. For taxi drivers, round the fare up to the nearest multiple of 10Sk (10 Slovak crowns) for a tip. Tip porters 20Sk per bag. Tour guides and concierges should be tipped between 20Sk and 30Sk for their services.

Slovenia

Tipping 10% is customary for especially good service in a restaurant, even when a service charge is added. Porters should be tipped SIT40 (40 tolars) per bag.

Taxi drivers don't expect a tip, but it's nice to round up the fare.

Spain

Tip waiters 10% for a full meal and 5% to 10% in smaller bars and cafés. Tip taxi drivers 5% to 10% of the meter if it's used. If a fare has been negotiated directly with the driver, no additional tip is necessary. Give train and airport porters €.50 per bag. Tip hotel porters and room service waiters €.50 to €1 per service, and maids €.60 per night for stays of two or more nights.

Sweden

The price of a meal generally includes a tip, but it's customary to tip waiters an extra 10% for exceptional service. Offer taxi drivers 10% of the fare. Tip hotel porters SKr 5 (5 kroner) per item. Most restaurants in Sweden require you to check your outerwear; for coatcheck people, leave SKr 10.

Switzerland

Although service charges are regularly included in bills at restaurants, a tip of 1SFr (1 Swiss franc) or 2SFr per person for a meal is fine, up to 10SFr for a first-class meal. Always tip waitstaff in cash. Give airport porters 5SFr per bag, and hotel porters and doormen 1SFr or 2SFr. Maids should be tipped 2SFr per night. Offer restroom attendants 1SFr as you leave. Tip ushers in theaters and at the opera 2SFr as you are seated.

Turkey

Leave an additional 10% tip above and beyond the service charge on restaurant bills. In top restaurants, leave an additional 10% to 15% for the waiter. Hotel porters should get the equivalent of between US$1 and US$4. Tip maids the equivalent of US$2 per night. For taxi drivers, round up the fare to the nearest 100,000TL (100,000 Turkish lira). Offer staff in Turkish baths 30% to 35% of the bill as you leave. Don't worry about going to find them, they'll make themselves available to you when you depart.

THE CARIBBEAN

All-inclusive resorts are popular vacation destinations in the Caribbean. While some of these resorts are truly all-inclusive—no tipping—some are not. Check with your travel agent or the resort management for individual resort tipping policies.

Anguilla

Hotels add a 10% service charge to the bill. This may or may not cover tips for staff, so ask the management if you're unsure whether or not to tip the hotel staff.

In restaurants, where a 10% service charge is usually added, no additional tip is needed, although it's perfectly appropriate to add 5% if you've had terrific service. Tip taxi drivers 10% of the fare.

Antigua

Hotels and restaurants add a 10% service charge to the bill. Tip waiters an additional 5% on top of that if you're very pleased with the service. Tip taxi drivers 10% of the fare. Porters and bellmen get the equivalent of US$1 per bag. Maids are rarely tipped, but you can give the equivalent of US$2 to US$3 per night if you've gotten exceptional service. At an all-inclusive resort, tipping isn't necessary, unless you'd like to recognize someone who went well out of his way for you.

Aruba

A service charge is commonly added to the bill, but porters and bellhops can be tipped US$2 per bag, and chambermaids US$2 per night. Restaurants usually add a 10% to 15% service charge to the bill, but if they don't, tip 10%. Leaving some small change for the waiter beyond the service charge is customary. Expect to tip a taxi driver 10% to 15% of the fare. U.S. dollars are accepted everywhere.

Bahamas

Hotels and restaurants will likely add a 15% gratuity to your bill, so no additional tipping is necessary. Tip porters US$1 per bag for their help. Tip taxi drivers 15% of the fare. The Bahamian dollar is on a par with and interchangeable with the U.S. dollar. Both currencies are acceptable.

Barbados

Restaurants and hotels commonly add a 10% service charge to their bills, so no extra tip is required unless you want to reward extraordinary service. If there is no charge added to a restaurant bill, tip the waiter 10% to 15%. Bellhops and airport porters can be tipped US$1 per bag, while maids receive US$1 per day. Taxi drivers get 10% of the fare for a tip.

Bonaire

Many hotels add a 10% to 15% maid service charge to your bill, therefore no tip is required beyond that. Tip bellhops US$1 per bag. Taxi drivers get a 10% tip. Most restaurants add a 10% to 12% service charge to the tab; leave a small additional tip for great service. If no charge is added to your bill, tip 10% to 12%.

British Virgin Islands

In restaurants a 10% charge may be added to the bill for service. Tip an additional 5% if the service was good or 15% when there is no service charge. Tip porters and bellhops US$1 per bag. Taxi drivers usually don't get a tip because they own their own cabs. You can add 10% to 15% of the fare if they've been particularly helpful.

Cayman Islands

A 15% tip in restaurants is the norm, but it may already be added as a service charge, so check your bill before tipping. In larger hotels, a service charge is commonly added, but in smaller establishments, tipping is up to you. Taxi drivers should be tipped 10% to 15% of the fare. Tip dive instructors CI$5 (5 Cayman Island dollars) to CI$10.

Cuba

Tip waiters between 10% and 20%. In buffet-style restaurants leave the equivalent of between US$2 and US$5 depending on the service you received and the number of people in your party. Tip hotel porters the equivalent of US$2 per bag and maids the equivalent of US$2 per day. Also tip taxi drivers, tour guides, and the person who keeps an eye on your rental car US$1 for their trouble.

Curaçao

Restaurants usually include a service charge so no additional tip is necessary. For very good service, you can add a tip of 5% to 10% on top of the charge. Porters and bellmen should receive US$1 per bag. Tip maids US$2 to US$4 per day. Tip a taxi up to 10%.

Dominica

Most hotels and restaurants add a 10% service charge to your bill. Add 5% as a tip when you're very pleased with the service. You don't need to tip a taxi driver as taxi rates are set by law and tips are not expected.

Dominican Republic

Restaurant checks and hotel bills commonly include a 10% service charge. If you've had exceptional service at a restaurant, you can add a 5% to 10% tip. Give maids RD$15 (15 Dominican pesos) per day for their services. Tip taxi drivers 10%—especially if they've helped with your bags. Skycaps and hotel porters should be tipped RD$10 per bag.

Grenada

If a restaurant or hotel doesn't include a 10% service charge in its bill, tip 10%. If it does add a 10% gratuity, no additional tip is necessary, though you can add 5% for especially good service. Tip taxi drivers 10% of the fare.

Guadeloupe

In restaurants a 15% gratuity is legally required to be added to the menu price, so you don't need to add a tip unless you want to reward excellent service. Hotel bills will usually include a 10% to 15% service charge. Tip skycaps and porters about €1 per bag. Most taxi drivers own their own cabs, so they don't expect a tip. If the driver doesn't own the cab, you'll be informed that a tip is expected—10% of the fare.

Jamaica

Hotels and restaurants generally include a 10% service charge. If they don't, tip between 10% and 20%, or as you would tip personnel in the United States. Cabbies customarily receive a 10% to 20% tip. Tipping is not allowed at the all-inclusive hotels in Jamaica.

Martinique

All restaurants in Martinique include a 15% service charge in the menu prices. No extra tip is necessary, unless you want to reward exceptional service. Quoted prices for hotel rooms include a 10% service charge, or one will be added to your total bill. No additional tip is needed although you should tip the bellhops and porters a few euros per bag. Most taxis are unmetered, so no tip is necessary beyond the agreed fare.

Puerto Rico

Some restaurants and hotels add a 10% to 15% service charge, so check your bill. If a charge has been added, it is customary to leave an additional 5% tip for the wait-staff, and if not, tip 15% to 20%. Hotel porters get US$1 per bag and maids should be tipped US$1 or US$2 per night. Tip taxi drivers 10% to 15% of the fare.

Saba

Hotel bills add a separate service charge or include the service charge in the room rate, but additional tipping of the hotel staff is customary. Tip chambermaids US$1 per day and bellhops US$1 per bag. Restaurants also add a 10% to 15% service charge, so no additional tip is necessary. If no service charge is added, tip 10% to 15%. Tip taxi drivers 10% to 15% of the fare.

St. Kitts and Nevis

A service charge of 10% is added to hotel bills, but you can tip the porters and bellhops US$1 per bag and housekeeping US$3 or US$4 a day. Tip taxi drivers 10% of the fare. A service charge may be added to a restaurant bill. If so, no additional tip is necessary. If not, tip 15%.

St. Lucia

Restaurants usually add a 10% service charge to the bill, so no additional tip is necessary. If a separate charge is not added for service, tip 10% to 12% of the tab. Porters and bellmen should be tipped US$1 per bag, unless you're at an all-inclusive resort with a no-tipping policy. Tip taxi drivers 10% to 12% of the fare.

St. Martin/St. Maarten

Service charges are included in hotel and restaurant prices or added to the bill separately, but an additional tip is still expected. Waiters should be tipped 10% to 15%. Porters get US$1 per bag and maids US$1 to US$5 per night. Taxi drivers usually receive a couple of dollars per trip.

St. Vincent and the Grenadines

Restaurants and hotels commonly add a 10% service charge to the bill. No other tip is expected, but you may want to reward excellent service. If no charge.is added, tip 10% of the bill. Taxi drivers do not expect tips.

Trinidad and Tobago

Most hotels include a 10% to 15% service charge; you don't need to tip beyond that. Restaurants also usually include a 10% service charge, but if not, tip between 10% and 15% of the bill. Tipping at bars is optional, and often the staff will tell you that you've forgotten your change when you leave it as a tip. Tip cab drivers 10% of the fare.

Turks and Caicos Islands

Hotels add a charge of 10% to 15% for service. Restaurants may do the same, but if not, tip 15% to the waitstaff. Tip taxi drivers 10% of the fare.

A SHORT HISTORY OF TIPPING

Tipping may date back to ancient Rome, where there are indications of money being paid for service above the cost of the service itself. Evidence also exists that in 16th-century England patrons would toss coins on the table to attract better service. Another theory holds that European feudal lords threw money to peasants in the streets to insure safe passage

As for the word "tip," the story goes that before the establishment of a postal service in England, ~~businessmen would give a shilling~~ to the courier "*to insure prompt service.*" Hence, the word "tip."

U.S. Virgin Islands

Many hotels include a 10% service charge, but that money may not all go to the staff. You can always ask a bellhop or a maid what they receive from the hotel management. If you need to tip more, tip porters and bellhops US$1 per bag and tip maids US$1 to US$2 per night. If you don't give a general tip beyond the service charge, be sure to tip for any special errands or requests you make of the hotel staff. Waiters should be tipped between 10% and 15% if no service charge has been added to the bill. Taxi drivers get 15% of the fare for a tip.

LATIN AMERICA

Argentina

In restaurants and bars add a 15% tip, and in casual cafés add 10%. Tip porters, doormen, and ushers at least $1 (1 peso). Taxi drivers don't necessarily expect a tip, but those who hang around hotels North Americans frequent will expect one. Round up the fare for your tip.

Belize

In Belize because a 10% service charge is included in your bill at restaurants and bars, no additional tip is necessary. Other service workers don't expect tips in Belize, but a small tip to hotel staff is nice. Cabbies don't expect any tips.

Bolivia

In restaurants tip the waitstaff 5% to 10%. Taxi drivers don't expect a tip, but if you hire one for the day, consider giving something extra. Give airport porters $b5 (5 bolivianos) for their service. Tip hotel porters $b5 for their help.

Brazil

If a 10% service charge is added to your restaurant bill, leave an additional 5% tip. When no service charge is added, tip 15%. In bars and cafés tip the same 15%, unless you order just coffee or a drink in an outdoor café. In deluxe hotels, tip porters R$2 (2 reals) per bag and maids R$2 per day. Tip porters at airports or train stations R$1 to R$2 per bag. Taxi drivers generally receive a tip of 10% of the fare. You may find yourself surrounded by children in the large cities looking for a handout. It's customary to "tip" them a quarter.

Chile

A 10% tip in restaurants is fine, though you may leave more for excellent service. Since most cabbies own their own cabs, they don't expect a tip. If you hire a cab for the day, however, consider adding a tip on top of the fare. Tip hotel porters, doormen, and ushers the equivalent of US$1 per service.

Colombia

A 10% service charge is usually added to your restaurant bill, so no tip is necessary. If a charge is not added, tip 10% to 15%. Hotels add a 16% service charge to your bill, but tip porters about 300 pesos per bag and maids the equivalent of US$2 or US$3 when you leave. Hotel clerks can be tipped 300 pesos. Taxi drivers don't expect tips.

Costa Rica

A 10% service charge is either included in the meal price or added to the bill in restaurants. There is no need to leave anything more, unless you want to reward great service. Hotel and airport porters should be tipped US25¢ to US50¢ per bag. Taxi drivers are usually not tipped. You can tip in American currency here.

Ecuador

In restaurants tip the waiter 5% to 10%, even if there is a service charge on the bill. Hotel porters and bellhops get the equivalent of US50¢ per bag. Tip guides the equivalent of US$4 to US$8 per person per day and drivers the equivalent of US$2 per person per day. Taxi drivers don't expect tips.

Guatemala

There is no service charge added to restaurant bills in Guatemala, so a tip of 10% is appropriate. Bellhops and maids expect tips only in the expensive hotels. If a guard or a local helps you find a place or gives you an impromptu tour, it's nice to give a tip for the help. Tipping taxi drivers is not expected.

Mexico

It is customary to tip your waiter 10% to 15% if a service charge hasn't been added to the bill. Give hotel porters and bellhops $10 (10 pesos) per bag, $20 per bag in expensive hotels. Tip maids $10 per night. Airport porters get $10 per bag. Tip tour guides and drivers at least $10 per person for a half- day tour. Give gas station attendants $5 to $10 if they do more than just fill your gas tank. Tip parking attendants and ushers $6 to $10, even if you've been charged for valet parking.

Nicaragua

Tip waiters 10% if no service charge has been added to the restaurant bill. Tip porters the equivalent of US$1 per bag and maids the equivalent of US50¢ per day. Do not tip taxi drivers.

Paraguay

A 10% tip for waiters is common. Tip more if you're really pleased with the service. Tip the same in bars, but if you're in a small local joint, just round up the bill to the nearest thousand guarani. In hotels tip the maids the equivalent of US$2 per day or US$5 to US$10 for a week's stay. Tip porters the equivalent of US50¢ per bag and doormen the same for hailing you a cab. At a gas station tip the attendant the equivalent of US30¢ for full service. Ushers and coatroom attendants get the equivalent of US10¢ to US30¢ per service.

Panama

Leave at least a 10% tip for the waitstaff in restaurants. Taxi drivers do not expect tips. Tip travel and hotel porters 50 centesimos per piece of luggage.

Peru

A 10% service charge is usually included in the meal price, but ask if you don't see it on the menu. If there is a charge, leave a modest 2% to 3%. If not, tip 5% to 10% on the pretax bill. When you're having a beer in a bar, leave between 20 centavos and 50 centavos, more for a mixed drink. Hotels may include a 10% service charge in the bill, but tip the porter US$1 per bag. Tip airport porters the same. Tip the washroom attendant 20 centavos. Tip tour guides and drivers 5sl (5 soles) to 10sl per day. Gas station attendants get a 50 centavo

tip if they wash your windows and such. Taxi drivers
do not expect tips.

Uruguay

A 10% tip to the waiter is customary in Uruguay.
When taking a cab, tip the driver by rounding up the
fare to the nearest peso. Tour guides get between $U5
(5 pesos) and $U10. Tip hotel porters $U1 per bag. Tip
doormen 50 centesimos.

Venezuela

Restaurants commonly add a 10% service charge, but
an additional tip of 10% is expected. Tip hotel porters
and tour guides from 500 Bs (500 Bolívares) up to 10%
of the tour, depending on the service. Taxi drivers
don't expect tips, but it's nice to offer a small one to a
driver who helps with your bags.

AUSTRALIA AND THE PACIFIC
Australia

Give waiters a 10% to 12% tip for good service. In hotels, although maids and room service staff are not
tipped unless they provide some extra service, you
should tip porters $A1 (1 Australian dollar) per bag.
Tour guides and drivers don't expect tips, but you can
contribute to a collection being taken in the group for

a tip. Taxi drivers don't expect tips, but leaving small change from your fare is nice.

New Zealand

Tipping is not customary in New Zealand. However, in better city hotels and restaurants a 10% tip for good service is appreciated.

Fiji

Tipping is not customary in Fiji; however, a donation to a staff fund at resorts will be accepted.

Tahiti

Tipping in Tahiti is not customary or expected.

AFRICA AND THE MIDDLE EAST

Morocco

Tip 10% of the bill in more formal restaurants, 5DH (5 dirhams) to 10DH per person in more informal cafés. Tip porters 5DH to 10DH, parking and washroom attendants 1DH to 2DH. Chambermaids should be tipped 5DH to 10DH per person per day. Give taxi drivers 1DH to 2DH.

South Africa

In South Africa tipping 10% in restaurants and bars is customary, unless a service charge has been added. Give taxi drivers and tour guide a 10% tip. Gas station attendants get R2 (2 rands) to R3 for washing your windshield and generally being helpful. Tip informal parking attendants in major cities R.50 to R2 for the service. Give porters should be given R1.5 to R2 per bag.

Egypt

Tipping is expected in Egypt. Be sure to carry plenty of 50p (50 piastre) and £E1 (1 pound) notes to pass around to taxi drivers, porters, doorkeepers, and others. You don't need to tip a lot—a small tip of £E1 to £E2 is fine. In a restaurant tip the waiter 10% of the check before taxes, even though checks include a 12% service charge. In luxury hotels tip porters £E10, and tip half of that in lower-scale hotels. Tip chambermaids £E5 for each visit. Tip room service waiters 10% of the total bill.

Israel

Even when a bill in a restaurant includes a service charge, an extra 10% tip is expected. Tip hotel bellhops a lump sum of IS8 (8 shekels) to IS15, not per bag. Taxi drivers don't expect a tip. Group tour guides usually receive IS20 to IS25 per person per day and the drivers receive about half that amount. Tip private guides IS82 to IS102 per day from the whole group.

Saudi Arabia

Make sure you carry plenty of change in Saudi Arabia, because many service people expect tips. Not much is required—a few coins are fine. Tip porters R5 (5 riyal) to R10. Because a service charge isn't commonly included in restaurant bills, tip waiters 10%, but be sure no charge has been added as a gratuity. It isn't necessary to tip cab drivers if you've negotiated a price with the gratuity included; otherwise, tip 10% of the fare.

ASIA

Brunei

In Brunei a 10% service charge is added to bills at hotels and restaurants, so no additional tip is necessary. Tip a hotel porter B$1 (1 Brunei dollar) per bag. If you've hired a car, tip the driver B$10 for a morning's ride. You don't need to tip taxi drivers.

China

Once not customary in China, tipping is slowly becoming a standard practice. In top-class restaurants, tip 8% of the bill. CTS tour guides are not allowed to accept tips, but you may consider giving a small gift such as American cigarettes or T-shirts, or, to a female guide, lipstick or nail polish.

Hong Kong

In Hong Kong a 10% service charge is normally added to a restaurant bill, and nothing more is called for. Tip bellhops and room service waiters Y10 (10 yuan) to Y20 or US$1 or US$2, as U.S. currency is always welcome for tips. You may leave the small change from your fare for a taxi ride, but tipping beyond that isn't necessary. In Hong Kong you'll be charged HK$5 (5 Hong Kong dollars) for every bag the taxi driver handles.

India

In general, India runs on tips, and Rs10 (10 rupees)—be it to a taxi driver, a doorman, or the shopkeeper's helper who carries your bulky goods to the car—go a long way in securing good service. Be sure to keep plenty of rupees to pass around throughout the day. In restaurants, tip the waiter 10%. Some hotels may include a service charge, but tip doormen, bellhops, and maids between Rs20 and Rs30. Tip room service waiters 10% of the check. Give airport and rail porters Rs5 to Rs10 per bag. Be sure to negotiate the tip before handing over your bags. Taxi drivers don't expect tips unless they go out of their way for you. If you hire a car and driver, tip Rs50 to Rs100 per day. Local guides you hire on the spot rate Rs40 for a half-day tour and Rs80 for a full day.

Indonesia

High-end hotels charge a 21% tax—part of which is a charge for various services. Beyond this, tip the bell-hop Rp10,800 (10,800 rupiahs) per bag. You need to tip the room service staff only if you're requesting some special service. Tip airport porters Rp5,400 per bag. Taxi drivers aren't tipped unless you're in Jakarta or Surabaya, where you tip Rp500 or the small change left from your fare. Tip a hired driver Rp21,000 for a half-day's work. Private guides may be tipped Rp21,600 for a half day and Rp54,000 for a full day. Most restaurants add a 10% service charge to the bill, but if not, a 5% to 10% tip is fine.

Japan

Tipping is generally not customary in Japan, but if you do tip, 10% is sufficient in restaurants with no added service charge. Commonly a service charge is added to a restaurant bill, and there is no reason to tip beyond that. You don't need to tip in bars or nightclubs, either. Nor do taxi drivers expect to be tipped, although hired chauffeurs may be tipped ¥00 (500 yen) for a half-day or ¥1000 for a full day. Porters in railway stations and airports charge for their service—from ¥200 to ¥300.

There is no need to tip employees in hotels, but if you feel you must, place a tip of ¥2000 or ¥3000 in an envelope and discreetly hand it to its intended recipient.

Malaysia

In Malaysia a 10% service charge is added to hotel and restaurant bills in establishments that are classified as tourist class. No tip is required beyond these charges. In nontourist-class establishments, no tip is expected. Tip airport porters M$1 (1 ringgit) per bag. You may tip taxi drivers with the coin change from your fare, but if you want to reward great service, a 10% tip is very generous.

Nepal

In most restaurants no tip is expected. Some upscale restaurants levy a 10% service charge; if your bill doesn't reflect this, tip 15%. A few rupees (Rs) are fine for a taxi driver unless he's driven a hard bargain for the fare. If you're on a camping trek, tip 200Rs per person per day. Give this to the guide in the presence of the other staff for a later ceremonious distribution to all the staff. When not on a camping trek, tip the guide 100Rs per person per day, and give 50Rs per day to the porter.

Philippines

Hotels and most restaurants add a 10% service charge to your bill; further tipping is optional, although it is customary to leave loose change. When there is no service charge, a 10% tip for a waiter is common. An airport porter expects P10 (10 pesos) for each bag, in addition to the P10 charged per cart that goes to the porter's office. Hotel doormen and bellhops get P10 per bag also. Tip a taxi driver P15 for a short ride.

Singapore

Tipping is not customary in Singapore and is prohibited at the airport. It is not expected in hotels, although you may give the bellhop S$1 (1 Singapore dollar) per bag if you wish. Tipping is also prohibited in restaurants, where a 10% service charge is added to the bill. As for taxi drivers, tipping is at your discretion—locals don't tip them.

Thailand

Tipping in hotels and restaurants is generally up to you, but some high-end establishments add a service charge to the bill. In restaurants if there's no service charge, tip waiters 10%. In hotels tip porters and other staff who have been attentive during your stay at least B20 (20 baht) at the end of your stay. In Bangkok tip taxi drivers by rounding the fare up to the nearest B5. Elsewhere, it's not necessary to tip taxi drivers unless you have hired them privately for an excursion.

Tibet

Some pricey hotels add a 15% service charge. However, tipping in Tibet is not customary.

Vietnam

Tipping in restaurants isn't customary. A service charge is always added to your check, and no further tipping is necessary unless you've had great service, in which case you might leave 5% to 10%. Small tips for bellhops and tour guides are appreciated, but the farther north you go, the more likely it will become that some hotel employees will refuse your tips. Taxi drivers expect tips, and sometimes help themselves out by telling you that they don't have the 2000D (2000 dong) or 5000D that you're expecting as change. It's up to you whether you argue for the change. Cyclo drivers should also receive small tips. They may ask for a "souvenir" after you've paid them, by which they mean a tip.

Check	15%	20%	Check	15%	20%
$1.00	$0.15	$0.20	$34.00	$5.10	$6.80
2.00	0.30	0.40	35.00	5.25	7.00
3.00	0.45	0.60	36.00	5.40	7.20
4.00	0.60	0.80	37.00	5.55	7.40
5.00	0.75	1.00	38.00	5.70	7.60
6.00	0.90	1.20	39.00	5.85	7.80
7.00	1.05	1.40	40.00	6.00	8.00
8.00	1.20	1.60	41.00	6.15	8.20
9.00	1.35	1.80	42.00	6.30	8.40
10.00	1.50	2.00	43.00	6.45	8.60
11.00	1.65	2.20	44.00	6.60	8.80
12.00	1.80	2.40	45.00	6.75	9.00
13.00	1.95	2.60	46.00	6.90	9.20
14.00	2.10	2.80	47.00	7.05	9.40
15.00	2.25	3.00	48.00	7.20	9.60
16.00	2.40	3.20	49.00	7.35	9.80
17.00	2.55	3.40	50.00	7.50	10.00
18.00	2.70	3.60	51.00	7.65	10.20
19.00	2.85	3.80	52.00	7.80	10.40
20.00	3.00	4.00	53.00	7.95	10.60
21.00	3.15	4.20	54.00	8.10	10.60
22.00	3.30	4.40	55.00	8.25	10.80
23.00	3.45	4.60	56.00	8.40	11.00
24.00	3.60	4.80	57.00	8.55	11.20
25.00	3.75	5.00	58.00	8.70	11.40
26.00	3.90	5.20	59.00	8.85	11.60
27.00	4.05	5.40	60.00	9.00	11.80
28.00	4.20	5.60	61.00	9.15	12.00
29.00	4.35	5.80	62.00	9.30	12.20
30.00	4.50	6.00	63.00	9.45	12.40
31.00	4.65	6.20	64.00	9.60	12.60
32.00	4.80	6.40	65.00	9.75	12.80
33.00	4.95	6.60	66.00	9.90	13.00

Check	15%	20%	Check	15%	20%
$67.00	$10.05	$13.20	$84.00	$12.60	$16.80
68.00	10.20	13.40	85.00	12.75	17.00
69.00	10.35	13.60	86.00	12.90	17.20
70.00	10.50	13.80	87.00	13.05	17.40
71.00	10.65	14.00	88.00	13.20	17.60
72.00	10.80	14.20	89.00	13.35	17.80
73.00	10.95	14.40	90.00	13.50	18.00
74.00	11.10	14.60	91.00	13.65	18.20
75.00	11.25	15.00	92.00	13.80	18.40
76.00	11.40	15.20	93.00	13.95	18.60
77.00	11.55	15.40	94.00	14.10	18.80
78.00	11.70	15.60	95.00	14.25	19.00
79.00	11.85	15.80	96.00	14.40	19.20
80.00	12.00	16.00	97.00	14.55	19.40
81.00	12.15	16.20	98.00	14.70	19.60
82.00	12.30	16.40	99.00	14.85	19.80
83.00	12.45	16.60	100.00	15.00	20.00

FYI Tipping Resources

FODOR'S RESOURCES

Guidebooks and References

A good guidebook always includes detailed tipping information.

Fodor's Gold Guides

Fodor's flagship series of guidebooks covers destinations around the world. Each volume includes detailed, up-to-the-minute information on the hundreds of places to stay, eat, and explore in that area, as well as solid tipping information and other points of etiquette.

Fodor's FYI Guides

If travel know-how is what you need, this series of slim books is for you. Simple and easy to read, they're packed with tips, hints, and checklists to keep you on track. Titles include *Plan Your Honeymoon, Travel with Your Baby, Plan &*

Enjoy Your Cruise, Travel Fit & Healthy, Fly Easy: How to Get There Safely, Comfortably, and Hassle-Free, and *Travel with Your Family,* about planning multigenerational trips and family reunions.

Fodor's Languages for Travelers

Need to know how to ask your questions in the language of the country? Check out *Fodor's French for Travelers, Fodor's German for Travelers, Fodor's Italian for Travelers,* and *Fodor's Spanish for Travelers.* For each title, there's a phrasebook/dictionary, along with a combination package that also includes either two audiocassettes or two CDs.

Online

fodors.com

If you don't find what you need in this book, search for "tipping" in the TravelTalk section of Fodor's website, or post a question of your own. Very often you'll get a solid answer within the day from a fellow traveler who has just been there, done that.

Crocodile Group

www.crocodile.org
Free download of BillSplit Palm Pilot software. Allows you to calculate a bill split with tip percentages.

Denton Software Group

www.dentonsoftware.com
Free Palm Pilot software for tipping calculations and hints. You may download from the site.

Magellan's

www.magellans.com
Online catalog for travel sites or you can call for a paper catalog. Offers a currency converter, a five-pocket purse for separating your money, and a travel wallet so that you'll always have your tip money handy.

The Original Tipping Page

www.tipping.org
Everything about tipping in the most complete online site.

U.S. Department of State

www.state.gov
The United States Department of State site that is filled with travel information, warnings, and cultural information for international travel.

XE.com

www.xe.com/euro.htm
A great site with loads of information about the euro. It has explanations, converters and links to other euro sites.

Notes

Notes

Notes

Notes

Notes